D1603032

Wildlings

Wildlings

by Mary Leister

photographs by Robert Wirth

STEMMER
HOUSE
PUBLISHERS, INC.

Owings Mills, Maryland
1976

The narratives collected in Wildlings *first appeared
in the Sunday* Sun, *Baltimore, Maryland*

Inquiries are to be directed to:

STEMMER HOUSE PUBLISHERS, INC.
2627 Caves Road, Owings Mills,
Maryland 21117

A Barbara Holdridge book
Printed and bound in the United States of America
First Edition

Library of Congress Cataloging in Publication Data

Leister, Mary.
  Wildlings.

  Essays originally written for the Baltimore Sun.
  1. Nature—Addresses, essays, lectures. I. Wirth,
Robert, 1923-II. Title.
QH81.L53   500.9'08   76-2063

To
Harold A. Williams, without whom...

Foreword

"If you would see something new under the sun, take the same path today that you took yesterday."

I don't know who said those words, nor where I read them, but I do know that they are true. For twelve years I have been walking the same countryside, day after day, learning to know it by foot and by heart, and the better I know it the more constantly I am surprised by the new things I see.

Only a small holding, within that square mile of Maryland farming country I claim as "my territory," actually bears my name on its legal title; but my neighbors, whom I deeply thank, have given me kind permission to ramble through their woods, fields and marshes, and upon the banks of their ponds; and to reap, without payment, the bountiful harvests of which the narratives in this book are but a sheaf held in one hand.

When I came to this area I thought eighteen acres of country land, that included a woods and a smidgeon of creek, would be ample territory to investigate with any thoroughness; but Kon-Tiki, my first Great Pyrenees, was a light-hearted, adventuresome friend who daily pushed our boundaries just a little further until she had expanded our domain to the square mile beyond which I refused to budge.

Reluctantly accepting this dictum, Tiki then proceeded to lead me into swamps and briar patches, through open woods, tangled thickets, overgrown pastures, and high-grown cornfields, introducing me, as far as she was able, to a dog's world of sights and sounds and textures and smells, and to a world of happenings I never would have experienced without her.

Kon-Tiki and I walked together for only a few short years. Kela, her successor, and as dear, is a steadier, more sedate companion. She is content to walk day after day in known areas, making the familiar more familiar, finding new and varied experiences in everyday terrain.

To this day there are no paths where we walk. Boots and briar-proof clothing are a necessity for me, and both of us must have the agility to climb over deadfalls, to slither under fences, to leap narrow, mud-bottomed streams, to climb hills and walk valleys in all weathers. For these and other reasons we walk happily alone.

For the sake of continuity I have used Kela's name in the narratives of this book, although, sometimes, it actually was Kon-Tiki who walked with me. But Tiki does not mind. As a happy shadow-dog she runs beside us still and shares our every mishap, our every adventure.

For the past four years our adventures have been published, month by month, in the Baltimore Sunday *Sun*. They are now arranged in chronological order in this book for another passage over the same territory and the possible discovery of "something new under the sun."

March 1976   —MARY LEISTER

With deepest thanks to Barbara Holdridge and to Mark Haller

Contents

The photographs on pages VI and 104
are by Virginia Hartman, and reproduced by permission.
The photographs on pages 1, 32, 86, 100, 120 and 151
are by Mary Leister.

Wildlings

True Voices of Spring

All this past winter, summer birds have lived about us. Flocks of robins have hopped with springtime insouciance across our fields and lawns. A pair of bluebirds has sheltered in the pine grove and even paid occasional investigative visits to bird houses along the orchard fence. A jaunty male towhee and a solemn brown thrasher have sustained themselves at our feeding station. Meadowlarks and cardinals, Bob Whites and mourning doves have whistled and called intermittently through all the cold months, and the song sparrows in the hedgerows have constantly trilled their summer-sounding music.

Songbirds, I've concluded, are delightful as birds, colorful and fascinating to study; but as harbingers of spring they are definitely not to be trusted. It's the early birds among the amphibians that tell us for certain when spring is on its way.

The spring peeper and the wood frog hibernating under the woodland mould know absolutely when the earth has warmed enough to stir their sluggish circulations back to life. Each one of them knows without question when he is alert enough to churn his way back to the world of light and air and water and other frogs.

When the season is early the frogs are early; when the season is late the frogs are late. There is no shilly-shallying about it. The frogs are honest prophets.

Spring peepers are usually given the honors for being first frogs at the pond; but as a general rule, wood frogs (and leopard frogs, too) have done their singing, their wooing, their mating, and gone back to the woods and off to the fields before the peepers have gotten their courtships properly started.

These spring rituals, though coming in their order, are often confusingly intermingled and overlapped; but there are years when they are celebrated separately and distinctly.

One afternoon, early in March, I heard, but could not

locate, a single spring peeper giving his clear *Preep, peep, peep* call from the edge of a broad, cold puddle in the swamp.

Then, as I approached my neighbor's pond, I distinctly heard the quacking of a great many ducks. Through binoculars I scanned the glassy surface. There was not a duck in sight, but half a dozen dark brown frogs floated there, heads up—and quacking. From under the water other voices called. Two of the surfaced males were clasping larger and lighter-colored females who plainly displayed their dark burglars' masks. Eastern wood frogs they definitely were. In three days they were gone, leaving behind them great jellied masses of eggs in the shallow water at the edges of the pond.

As the wood frogs left the pond the leopard frogs took over, coming up from the mud and detritus of the bottom where they had spent the winter. They hung in the water with bright eyes and vocal pouches just above its surface; but their voices were a soft, moaning, throaty sound, almost a talking, and so low that only the person who waits at the pond, listening with his skin, ever experiences that vibrant murmur.

But only one day of hazy warmth was given over to the leopard frogs, for now, third in line, came the spring peeper chorus. Each day, as the earth grew warmer, a few more of the tiny creatures had gathered at the edges of scattered ponds and puddles, and, suddenly, like thousands upon thousands of chiming silver sleigh bells, their voices rang across the countryside.

Spring peeper voices ring so loudly it is almost impossible to believe the singers can be so small. As a youngster, I remember, I looked for peepers fruitlessly, season after season, until at last, I seriously looked at a ruler and saw how small three-quarters of an inch really is.

Nowadays I find it helps to pretend I am looking for an insect, not a frog, in the grasses, weeds and mosses around the water, and every year I am astonished again at the miniature perfection of the first tiny peeper I see.

Peepers vary in color through several shades of brown, from light to dark and from yellow-brown to ash-brown, and each one wears an irregular, attenuated X across his back. They blend perfectly with the brown and tawny grasses and scarcely show against the greener moss.

As for their eggs, I wondered for years why I could never find a single jellied mass in any of the swamp ponds where so much singing and obvious mating had been going on. The answer, so lately learned, is patent and three-fold. Their eggs are the size of tiny seeds, one-fifteenth of an inch in diameter. They lay them one by one. They drop them all over the bottom of the pond.

Although the female is larger (an inch to an inch-and-a-quarter long), it is always a male I see first—for a good reason. He is doing the singing. The sound of his piping is ventriloquistic, but it still helps in locating him, for it narrows the field to a square yard or so. What always catches my eye and pinpoints his position is the glistening, transparent bubble beneath his chin.

This glistening bubble is his expanded vocal sac and it is almost as big as the peeper himself. His mouth is closed and he vibrates his vocal chords by moving the air back and forth between his lungs and the sac.

Only the male sings at breeding time. His singing entices the female to the pond. Her slight movement at his side stimulates him to leap upon her back, clasp her tightly under the arms, and be carried by her into the water—where she does the swimming for both of them for the three days to nearly a month it may take until the eggs are shed and fertilized.

But if you think procreation is the only thing on the male's mind you must visit a pond on a warm and humid evening when courtship is in full tilt, and notice how many times a female may find it necessary to nudge her ardent suitor away from his singing.

For male peepers sing in trios, it appears; each one, in turn, singing solo. The peeper chorus at the pond is made up of dozens or hundreds of these trios singing without a leader and apparently making up complex patterns of rising and falling volume as they go along. Each singer is attentive to the sound, as men singing close harmony listen to each other, and they possibly become mesmerized by the polyphony they are creating.

Why do frogs sing? For the same reason that birds and people sing: They feel good. The singing does entice a mate, but that is nature eternally seeking to perpetuate the species.

These frogs have come through five cold months spent in total darkness at a pinpoint of existence barely this side of death. Now they are back in a world of food and warmth and light— and they can't keep quiet about it.

And that's as good a reason and as true a voice of spring as any I know.

The Chaos of April

Once again the clockwork precision of an ordered universe swings our hemisphere of Earth into the clamoring chaos of topsy-turvy April.

Every living thing, plant and animal, marsh and field, meadow and woodland, is swelling, bursting, stretching, standing tiptoe, caught up once more in the heady excitement of becoming. For April is a thirty-day passage, brimful of activity, random and haphazard, standing between the fitful promises of March and the warm fulfillment that is May.

Frost is only an early morning dust on the surface of these humming days. The stiffness is gone from the earth and fresh life juices are percolating upward. Hair-thin roots are lengthening, reaching into commissary darkness. New green and red and purple shoots of a thousand kinds are thrusting their noses into the sunlight.

Ferns unroll their furry fiddleheads. Spice bushes open misty yellow blooms. Bloodroot daisies poke rounded noses from the shelter of close-wrapped leaves. Pussytoes show velvet fuzz just above the ground. Maples and willows brush a haze of red and yellow along lanes and waterways. First wild ginger. First anemones. First upthrust cones of purpled preacher-Jack.

Honeybees buzz between meadow and hive with basketloads of pollen from powdery catkins of pussy willow, hazel bush, and water-loving alder. Famine time is over. The feasting time of nectar-flow is about to begin. Hive walls must be refurbished and winter cracks filled in, and young apprentice bees are sent out to collect "bee gum" from the outer edges of swelling leaf and flower buds.

Bumblebee queens in black and yellow "fur" fly low to the ground inspecting every cranny. Each one seeks a cozy cavern where she can build a honey pot, brood a batch of eggs, and get her season's colony started.

On the tips of wild cherry twigs hosts of almost-micro-scopic caterpillars chew themselves free of dark-shelled eggs. Heads against heels they make their way, single file, down the branch until they reach a spot pleasing to the first-born cater-pillar in the lead. All together they stretch their silken guy lines. All together they produce and spread the fine white gossamer of their first small tent.

Earthworms unwind themselves from the soft red masses of their fellows and crawl upward from their dark hibernacula below the frostline of the earth. Eating, digesting, refining organic materials as they go, they spread fresh rich earth behind them. At the rain-wet surface, they face the hard yellow bill of the robin and the sharp white teeth of the skunk.

Mourning cloak butterflies creep from their winter hiding places and drift about the woods on strong, dark wings. White cabbage butterflies, breaking out of their chrysalis prisons, float in chosen places like animated clouds. And tiny, dainty azures find incongruous delight in the yellow stickiness of a muddy puddle.

Flocks of robins, flocks of geese, flocks of swans, and flocks of ducks. But when did the juncos disappear? When did the last of the white throats leave us? And the fox sparrows? And the evening grosbeaks? The tree sparrows are gone and the chipping sparrows are here. When did one replace the other?

Ecstatic cardinal and blue jay males are carrying bits of food to the mates who for the rest of the year had jolly well better take care of themselves. In the deepening twilight the male woodcock pursues his courtships with an aerial song and dance entrancing to the ear.

In the algaed puddles of the marshes and on the margins of deeper ponds, frogs and peepers are still singing, courting, and laying jellied eggs. March-laid eggs are hatching into tad-poles. Tadpole heads and mouths are changing. Tadpole bodies are sprouting legs. Tadpole creatures are turning into frogs. And there are more to come. Green frogs, bull frogs and squatty toads with pretty voices will scarcely reach the ponds before the last week of the month.

On the surface of the pond, over-wintered whirligig beetles circle dizzily. Water boatmen, upside down, row intermittently through the warming days, stocking oxygen for underwater needs. And groups of long-legged water-striders press small dimples into the water as they skate in search of strider mates and tiny, elusive insect prey.

Cloudy schools of fingerlings dart from sunny shallows into darker pools when a passing shadow falls across them, but dark-shelled snails lining up for hermaphroditic rites are unaware.

Mud-coiled castles built by thin-shelled crayfish appear overnight along the edges of ponds and creeks and in the wetness of the marshes. On another day, demolished castles and a scattering of raccoon tracks tell of succulent crayfish served for family dinner.

Raccoons are creatures of the night, and it is only upon occasion that the early morning sun finds a big old male clambering up his den tree or a mature female, heavy with this year's brood, hurrying her yearlings into the maze of old burrows around an outcropping of gray granite rock.

Opossums, though, are all about, wandering without apparent destination through the pale beginnings and endings of almost every April day. They forage, usually singly, but sometimes by twos and threes, for newly-stirring beetles and snails, for spiders and millipedes and fiery-tempered shrews. The female opossum walks with ponderous care, for the eight or ten babies secluded in her pouch make her movements awkward and slow.

Female skunks, too, move heavily through early evening and dark-time hours, for many of them will bear their young in the latter days of April. But slim gray squirrels scamper briskly up the white oaks and vanish into hollow limbs or leafy nests placed high among the branches, there to attend their ever-hungry nurslings.

Blind and naked baby rabbits fill shallow, grass-and-fur-lined nests on practically every open hillside. They are the prey of almost everything that moves; yet some of them always, miraculously, survive to hide in briar patches, to nibble pasture grasses, and to spring lightly over the ground with jaunty white powder puffs flashing behind them.

Free as a Bird?

The month of May is for the birds. Its lilac-fragrant air vibrates with the sounds of their voices, is filled with the busyness of their comings and goings, streams to the sweep of their feathered wings. It's a clamorous, purposeful, hurry-scurry season. Summer residents and year-arounders alike are caught up in a tidal flow of irresistible instinct.

Every male must find and hold a territory. Every female must find an established male and approve both him and the area he has selected. Together they must choose a nesting site, find materials for nest-building, construct a nest, mate, produce eggs, brood, feed the hatchlings, clean the nest, drive off intruders, get the youngsters out of the nest, teach them to feed, to fly, and to fend for themselves.

There are species variations on the general theme, but for all the pace is breathless. And not one of them can say "no" at any stage of the process. Not one of them can drop out and watch the show from the sidelines.

And yet, within the confines of this inescapable pattern, many birds find a certain freedom of choice, especially in the choosing of a nesting site.

Flickers, for instance, can chip out their own nesting holes in true woodpecker fashion, but they will also use natural woodland cavities whenever they can find them; or they will nest in long boxes attached to fence posts in open fields; or they will scoop out depressions in bare earth and deposit their white and shiny eggs on the ground.

Chickadees, too, will excavate their own homes in rotten tree stumps or decaying fence posts if any are available. If not, they will use old woodpecker holes or proper bird houses placed by thoughtful human beings.

Gregarious redwings, accustomed to congregating in swamps and marshes, build just as often in grain and hay fields that may be half a mile from a water supply. House wrens are notorious for building in anything from tin cans to coat pockets, to straw hats or wash basins. And robins will place their nests just about anywhere except on the ground.

Robins will build thirty feet up on a window ledge or four feet above the orchard grasses in a leaning apple tree. They will build on any convenient projection inside or outside any kind of building, and they have an apparent predilection for construction sites. Automobiles, locomotives and airplanes have all been halted by a pair of bright, beady eyes peering fearlessly (or trustingly, or possessively) over the side of an egg-filled nest.

But is there, just possibly, a limit even to a robin's freedom in nest placement? Is it just possible that the bird community will police a really flagrant disregard for family security?

Last May, a young female robin chose to place her nest twenty feet up on the northwest side of a slender wildcherry tree exposed to the edge of the lawn. She built precariously in the angle formed by the only two branches growing from the trunk on that weather-beaten side of the tree.

Her mate tried to dissuade her, leading her off to more suitable spots in lawn trees and orchard. She would have none of them. She gathered straw from the garden and twigs from the woods floor and fashioned the outside bowl of her nest while directing a string of unceasing invective at her mate who sat silently drooping in a red oak close by.

When the framework was completed, she flew off to gather mud and her mate trailed along behind her.

While they were gone a pair of blue jays flew in and, with a great deal of noise, tore the straw nest from its moorings and left it dangling down the trunk.

For two days the female robin followed her mate as he flew from one desirable nesting site to another, but at the end of that time, with her first nest dangling below her, she began to rebuild on her original spot.

Again her mate moped and again she scolded while she gathered materials and rebuilt the nest and fought off the two blue jays who now attacked directly. Her mate joined her in the fighting, but, again, when the robins flew off to the marsh the

jays tore the nest loose and left it dangling down the tree just above the frayed remains of the first nest.

This time, the female wasted no time looking at other sites. She started right in to rebuild. The male, giving in, brought her a piece of straw. She snatched it from him and gave him a vocal drubbing and he brought no more. But together they fought the blue jays. He stayed at the nest, battling, while she made trip after trip to bring mud from the creek bank. She lined the nest with soft, dry grass.

Then, for two successive sunny days the blue jays kept to themselves. The two robins mated, and mated yet again on the lawn a short distance from the nest tree, and the female spent a great part of those two free days sitting on her nest, exposed to all the eyes in the vicinity.

And suddenly the two robins were fighting off a host of hostile birds. Four bluejays came screaming to the attack. A pair of starlings joined the fray. Two mockingbirds, two catbirds, two brown thrashers, a grackle and a cardinal. All came crying, diving, swooping, pecking. They attacked by ones, by twos, by sixes; and the robins, armed with territorial righteousness, held them off.

It was more a war of nerves and noise than of actual physical combat, but it was a prolonged and unequal fight. On the twentieth day following the two-day truce, the robins abandoned their nest in the wildcherry tree. They dropped away from their besieging neighbors, flew like two shadows across the lawn and garden, and disappeared into the full-leafed orchard.

There, while their erstwhile enemies went quietly back to their own affairs, the two robins built a standard robin nest in the regulation snugness of a well-branched apple tree, and reared four healthy youngsters without a single instance of interference from the neighborhood vigilantes.

Glowworms in Sawdust

Many years ago a sawmill stood on this rise above the gurgling confluence of two small streams. One by one the great white oaks, maples and hickories of the surrounding woods passed through its whining teeth and became wide boards for the building trades, and the fragrant dust of their cutting piled in ever-growing cones below the mill.

Now the sawmill has vanished, along with the giant trees, and only low heaps of rotted sawdust and a clearing still resistant to encroaching second-growth marks the spot where it stood.

On a sunny morning in June I knelt in this clearing, in the shade of wild cherry saplings, and scratched carefully into the damp margins of an old sawdust mound. I was not looking for anything in particular and was just as conscious of the perfume of honeysuckle pervading the clearing, of a catbird scolding from the greenbriers, of a box turtle swaying, tall on his legs, beneath the Mayapple umbrellas, as I was of the sawdust into which I dug.

Slugs and earthworms, centipedes and sow bugs were plentiful there, and as I disturbed the grasses on the sawdust margins, three fragile black fireflies lifted into the air on their dark chiffon wings and disappeared among the lower branches of the trees.

These fireflies (*Photinus pyralis*) often drift about in the daylight hours, especially when their sleeping quarters are invaded, so I watched them go without surprise and thought how strongly they contrasted with their great, hard-shelled, careening cousins, *Photuris pennsylvanica*, which I have never seen in daylight hours though they frequent the same areas.

And the very next flip of my exploring fingers brought a glowworm, the larva of a firefly, up to the surface. Dark and flattened, and seeming armor-plated, he crawled over the wet sawdust on his thin legs, dug himself down into its upper layer, and hid in the dark again.

I pulled my ever-present lens from my jeans pocket and rudely disinterred the secretive glowworm. He was more than half an inch long, nearly ready to pupate and to emerge, this very summer, as a sparkling, free-soaring firefly.

Through my glass I could see his peculiar tail, like a tuft of little strings, and it seemed he propelled himself as much by pushing from behind with those bristly filaments as by walking on his short, thin legs. But, even with the lens, I could scarcely see the two round lights beneath his body near his tail. I cupped my hand about him to deepen the shadows and his lights glowed with tiny intensity.

He poked his dark, pin-top head from under its oversize shield and I had a good look at his curved mandibles, so lethal to earthworms, slugs and other soft-bodied animals. I knew, but could not see, that those piercing mandibles were hollow tubes through which the glowworm squeezes a poison into the bodies of his captured prey, turning them to a liquid which he can drink through the narrow vein that is his throat.

I watched this strange little creature for a while and then allowed him to dig himself back into the sawdust while I did some more exploratory digging of my own. I was so interested now in the possible contents of the sawdust that I scarcely heard the falsetto voice of the towhee struggling to sing a proper "Drink your tea!," and paid very little attention to the small wasp who fussed endlessly over the half-dozen cells in her paper cone under the blackberry leaves.

In the hour or so that I spent at my "dig" I unearthed glowworms of practically every size from not quite one-quarter inch to almost three-quarters inch long, each with its two tiny tail-lights impractically aglow and its helpful fringe-tail pushing it along; but not one of them telling me to which species he belonged.

The quarter-inch glowworms puzzled me at first, for I thought they were of the present season's hatching, and that would seem to play havoc even with Nature's slightly elastic time tables. Four weeks, give or take a day or two, is the established period from new-laid egg to baby glowworm, and I think

I have never seen a firefly flashing in this area before the final week of May. Perplexed by the too-speedy appearance of these tiny glowworms, I finally realized that they had hatched in the fall from final batches of last summer's eggs and had grown but little before hibernating—and nature's Rules of Order settled into place again.

Thinking then of firefly eggs, which I had never seen, I considered that thousands of them had been laid, already this season, in and about that clearing in the woods. Many a female firefly, I thought, would find it easy to penetrate the loose-textured surface of the sawdust with her ovipositor, or, depending on her species, simply to drop her tiny eggs there. I could easily search the sawdust for the firefly eggs I could never hope to find in a grassy meadow.

Well, the searching was easy but the finding was hard. With greatest care I scraped away the surface of the sawdust; then, minutely, through the lens, I scanned both the sawdust I removed and the spot from which I removed it. Over and over and over again—and no eggs.

I knew the eggs were tiny and that they were planted or dropped one at a time while the female, either afoot or drifting close to the ground, wandered about. But I thought the yellow color of even a single egg would show up well against the dark dampness of the old sawdust.

And it did show up, but not very well, and not until I realized that the fireflies would stay hidden and lay their eggs among the familiar grasses growing in the low margins of the sawdust piles, not up on the exposed and sloping sides of the mounds.

Even so, I found only two minute specks of yellow in those grassy margins, round and smooth, with a suggestion of transparency and of vulnerability as though the careless pressure of a fingertip could crush them. But I could not be certain they were firefly eggs, or even eggs at all, until, magnified seven times under my doubled lens, one of them showed the faintest hint of a firefly glow—from the two round tail-lights of the little glowworm developing within.

The Seamy Side of Summer

"Those nature walks of yours sound heavenly," an acquaintance remarked the other day. "Doesn't anything bad ever happen? Aren't there any snakes? Isn't there any poison ivy?"

Of course there is poison ivy, great clumps of it. It grows around every outcropping of rock on the hillsides, and there are formidable hedges of it along the borders of the woods. Low thickets of it grow inside the woods too, and its vining form climbs occasional trees to a height of twenty feet or more. It grows in fields, in gardens, in flower beds. I can't possibly avoid it.

Somewhere along the line I lost my childhood immunity to its poison, but I have discovered that a sponge bath with cold vinegar water, and no toweling off, every day before going out of doors, almost completely frees me from poisoning. If, in spite of the vinegar, a blister pops up on my skin, I keep it covered with baby oil to eliminate the itching, and the blister is gone in a week. So much for poison ivy.

And of course there are snakes. There are even supposed to be a few copperheads around, but in all my wandering and in all my gardening I have never seen one, and I shall be quite happy if I never do.

As for other kinds of snakes, non-poisonous kinds, I so rarely see one that I'm apt to forget they exist. Even when one does glide across my path he disappears so swiftly that I have little chance to identify him, except, sometimes, to recognize the family to which he belongs.

Even a captive snake or a dead snake isn't always easy to identify. I sat in the middle of our road (little traveled, obviously) for twenty minutes one morning, field guide in hand, trying to decide whether a snake killed by a car was a corn snake, a fox snake or a milk snake. It turned out to be a corn snake. Fox snakes don't live in this area, and milk snakes have somewhat different markings on head and neck. Besides, milk snakes have smooth scales and a single anal plate while corn snakes have weakly keeled scales and divided anal plates. But I couldn't use that information because this was the first snake I'd ever tried to identify in this manner and I wasn't sure I knew what a keeled scale or an anal plate was.

Actually a black racer in the woods or a garter snake on the lawn is practically my only contact with the serpent clan.

So snakes are no problem, but deer flies are. Hordes of those blood-starved insects infest the woodlands throughout the summer months and torture unmercifully any warm-blooded creature who ventures into their domain. Even one deer fly circling your head is nerve-wracking, but when ten or twenty or fifty of them threaten and buzz it is maddening. The flies are out for blood, of course, and each bite is like a jab with a burning needle. The spot itches for hours, and sometimes for days.

When Kela and I walk through the woods her body is protected by her thick white coat, but the flies attack the short-haired areas of her face and her legs. I wear long sleeves, heavy cotton gloves, slacks and boots, and my head is swathed in a scarf that protects my neck, too. But if the scarf is stretched over my head, the flies bite through it; if it is tied loosely, they crawl inside where it is cozy to bite. If my blouse or jacket lies closely across my shoulders they bite there, too. But the flies aren't anything "bad." They are just a discomfort.

We have, though, two or three times, gotten ourselves into sticky situations with domestic cattle and horses where the outcome could have been serious. We managed one way or another to escape with whole skins.

There are no pathways where we walk, and in summer we wade through green growth of differing heights and densities. In one particular field, from July on, we push our way through thick vegetation, mostly late goldenrod, that is higher than my head. Now and again I may stumble over a hidden stone or drop without warning into the open doorway of a groundhog hole. I have stepped into yellowjacket nests or brushed against the pendant discs of paper wasps and been stung for my clumsiness. But the field is a jungle of summertime flowers and I cannot let a chance encounter with an angry insect keep me out of it.

So—all of our walks are not exactly heavenly. I find this entry in my journal for one particularly humid summer morning:

"The sun is hidden behind the hills, still half an hour from rising, but already Kela is panting heavily as she wades ahead of me through the marsh. The morning air wraps about us, tangible, hot, and sticky. We breathe warm steam into our nostrils. I am bathed in perspiration. It drips from my chin, meanders about the roots of my hair, trickles down my back, and creeps like oversize gnats across the backs of my knees.

"The soupy bottom of the marsh sucks at our feet and drags upon our footsteps. Kela leaps at a frog among the reeds. She lands heavily. Thick black water spurts into the air, spatters my hair, my clothes, my face. Kela's hair, white and shining when we left the house, is splashed with mud and knotted with burs.

"Sedge grass and bur reeds slap at my waist; horse nettles and tear thumb clutch at my knees; long silver thistle spines puncture my skin wherever they touch. I turn a wary eye to a steer on the bank and the thorns of a greenbrier rip across my shoulders.

"Mosquitoes whine in our ears. Gray gnats torment our noses and our eyes. Deer flies buzz about our heads. We are miserable with heat and bugs and mud.

"But nobody forced us to come out here today. It's just that it's morning, and this is our world, and we find peculiar pleasure even in the occasional miseries it provides."

The Enchanted Frog

At the bottom of the cornfield two mulberry trees and a maple grow in a triangle, leaning toward one another so that their heads touch and their leaves and branches intermingle. Multiflora roses and greenbriers with wicked thorns grow thickly about their bases, and rampant honeysuckle fills any space the briers leave unoccupied.

It looks rather like the ramparts of the Sleeping Beauty's castle during the years the princess lay asleep; but at its center lies, not a bedroom, but a spring that has been abandoned for several years.

For more than a hundred years this spring supplied water for a succession of tenant families living in the brown house two good stone-throws away. Before that it quenched the thirsts of field hands, and before that it doubtless served both wandering Indian and sojourning wild animal.

It is still a watering place for small animals who creep beneath the thorny barriers; but the old house is tenanted only by termites, and the men who till the rented fields do so in massive machines, glass-enclosed and air-conditioned, and they bring their own brands of liquid refreshment in tinkling thermos jugs. So no human foot has kept a pathway open to the spring, and the growth about it has become thicker and more forbidding with every passing year.

But Kela and I found our way through the Castle's impenetrable wall. Or, more truthfully, Kela found the way and I followed.

On a hot August afternoon we turned from the main creek and waded a rivulet that trickled between the grass-covered banks of an interesting side channel. At the edge of the pasture we crept beneath a rusted barbed wire fence, crawled almost flat under a shield of greenbrier and honeysuckle, crushed the watery stems of a stand of jewel weed growing directly in the water, blinked our eyes and stood quite still in a cave of cool green darkness.

Actually it wasn't dark in there; it only seemed so after the burning sunlight of the meadow. This place was filled with light—soft, trembling, green-washed light—that filtered through the leaves. It was not lofty enough nor vast enough to be a castle, but it was an airy room, friendly and sheltering.

We splashed to the edge of the spring and I reclined against its mossy banks while Kela gamboled in the small pool at the head of the runoff. Between the spring and the pool someone had laid a bridge, a small openwork construction from which it would be easy to dip water pails or to kneel for long cooling draughts.

The bridge had been placed there a long time ago. Its supports were rotted away and it lay with its undersurface touching the water. Kela found it a great takeoff point for splashing plunges into the little pool and I discovered that I could sit on the bank with my feet comfortably propped against the bridge and muse for half-hours at a time.

By all rights there should have been mosquitoes and flies in so sheltered a spot, but there were none. This was a sanctuary, a place of joy and solitude unspoiled by anything.

This cool, moist retreat has been the secret mecca of our August afternoons. I don't know how many visits we had already made, nor for how many of those visits I might have overlooked the green frog squatting in a frog-sized niche at my elbow; but one sunny day there he sat, completely unperturbed by either Kela's noisy splashing or by my reclining practically against him.

A sunbeam shone through a parting of the mulberry leaves directly on the niche where the green frog sat, warming him and glinting on the spots of gold that freckled his green head and shoulders. Two brown lines flecked with gold dust marked the ridges on either side of his back. The lower part of his body, and his arms, and his legs as well, were mottled brown, and his throat was a clear bright yellow. He was a pretty fellow, and he sat there calmly as a Buddha while Kela played at her watery sports. He was still there a half-hour later when we crept out beneath the curtain of greenbriers, and left the spring and the frog behind.

The next day at very nearly the same hour we were back at the spring, and there was the frog ensconced in his niche. And the next day and the next day and the next day we were there and so was the frog. I spoke to him each day but he did not answer. No motion of mine disturbed him, and Kela, romping and barking in the water, did not exist. The frog blinked his eyes and the pulse in his throat pumped visibly. Otherwise he did not stir.

On the fifth day, after sitting beside him and making a few unanswered conversational remarks for some minutes, I gently touched him with one finger. He did not move. I stroked his gold-sprinkled back. He blinked and sat on. His skin felt soft and cool to my touch. Over and over I stroked his sides. Did I imagine it or did he press, ever so slightly, against my finger?

"Why, this frog is enchanted!" I thought. "If I lean over, now, and kiss him on his flat green nose, he will turn into a handsome prince."

But I didn't do it. And the next day when Kela and I sought our green-lighted retreat, the niche in the bank was empty. I checked every inch of those mossy banks, and Kela certainly explored the water, but the frog was not there.

He never has reappeared, and I keep wondering. . . .

A Month of Beginnings

"What would the world be without wildness and wet?" I gaily misquoted as Kela and I plunged into the head-high wealth of September weeds. The words ended on a high note as a chill tippling of dew from a goldenrod cascaded between open collar and nape of neck and trickled down my back.

It was only the first of a hundred impromptu showers, the first of countless leaves that brushed us with wetness as we threaded the tall growth. By the time we reached the creek Kela's white coat had lost its fluff and my shirt and jeans were plastered to my skin. By this time, too, our bodies were warmed with exertion and fun, and the green sea we walked in was cool and refreshing.

Cool, refreshing, and colorful. Above the wet greenness were the gold of sunflower and goldenrod, the purple of ironweed and aster, the blue of chicory, the yellow of meadow lilies, and the freckled oranges and bronzes of the Turk's caps. But the edge was off the show, I realized; its brilliance was definitely fading. The dainty heads of Queen Anne's lace were curling into bird's nests, the fluffy purples of Joe Pye blooms were browning steadily, and there were more ripening pods than blossoms on every plant in the field. The spice-toned flowers of autumn were definitely going to seed.

The realization brought no sigh of sadness from me, for there's as much excitement in the ripenings of autumn as in the tingling sap-rises of spring, and as much to be sought and absorbed in the ending as there is to be discovered and learned in the beginning. But, even so, the noting of the signs can be sudden and disconcerting.

We splashed along the swampy edge between the quiet field and the woods noisy with the cries of jays and the rattle, bump and crack of hickory nuts bouncing down limbs and branches to the leaf-carpeted floor. These were not ripe hickory nuts falling of their own ripeness but fat ones being cut down by chattering squirrels eager for the harvest. And the smell from the woods and the fields was a mellow, pungent scent of leaves and seeds and flowers and earth in rich stages of fulfillment.

We climbed the steep rise at the corner of the woods and I noted the bristled burs of the burdocks and the long nodding beards of the fox-tail grasses, and the fact that no swallows swooped over our heads to gather the insects scared up by our passing. The summer of the swallows was over, the sweeping flights were gone, and the field at the top of the hill lay all in sharp stubble from the last hay crop of the season.

We had scarcely stepped into this stubble when a male Bob White, white of face and dark of bill, fluttered just ahead of us, then dropped to the ground and staggered toward the edge of the field uttering little agonized cries. He held his wings tightly to his body but his little rear drooped, and he dragged it so painfully across the stubble that I wondered if he might have caught some birdshot from the dove hunters who throng the cornfields every afternoon.

But no sooner had the little fellow reached the shelter of a fence corner than his voice subtly changed, and, about our feet, the hay stubble came alive with fifteen baby Bob Whites swarming like earth-bound, brown bumblebees toward the honey-suckle tangle where good old papa awaited them, crooning now, a sweet-toned series of untranslatable syllables that apparently meant plenty to those scrambling babies.

I laughed. I laughed at the busyness of those tiny chicks in the hampering stubble, and at myself, in chagrin, for having been taken in by the ruse of the parent bird. In self-defense, though, I have to say I was thrown off guard by seeing only the male parent, and I was scarcely expecting to see such newly-hatched chicks in September.

Kela and I ran along our own narrow path through a purpling bramble patch and crept under the barbed wire into the pasture. We struck off across the ravine, and on its far bank Kela stopped to sniff at a tuft of dry grass. Something leaped within it, hitting against the grass, and Kela drew back, startled by the movement. She sniffed again, then thrust her black nose into the grass, pushing it apart and exposing a nestful of baby rabbits. Three of them lay curled deep within the nest but the fourth one leaped to touch Kela's nose. His eyes were open—I would guess they had just opened—and he must have thought the animal nuzzling through the nest grasses was his mother. Kela responded by licking the little rabbit maternally with her big wet tongue.

I pulled her away before she could assume ownership of the nest and we went on with our walk, Kela hankering to go back to the rabbits and I wondering what the mother would do when she found her nest smelling so dreadfully of dog.

At the gray rocks under the maple trees we frightened a brood of half-grown pheasants, four young hens and three young roosters, looking ragged and rusty in their half-feathered state. They looked awkward, too, in their long-legged, helter-skelter running, but they disappeared swiftly into the green-seeded ragweeds and we saw them no more.

Walking softly on the mosses of our own woods-road, we were scolded by gray squirrels on every hand, and I knew that in at least two of the leafy nests and in one hollow limb tiny squirrels were snuggled in sleeping babyhood.

What a month of beginnings September is, I suddenly thought—with baby birds and baby rabbits and baby squirrels. And seeds. You can't get much closer to beginnings than seeds.

Turtle Trouble

ay by day and week by week, autumn's coloring leaves and lowering temperatures proclaimed a coming frost. Now, on this clear October morning, our thermometer registered a cool thirty-eight degrees, and the lawn, as we crossed it, lay crisp and white under the first frosty coat of the season.

The woods were noisy with the clatter of falling nuts and acorns, the rustle and slap of jettisoned leaves, the chatter and scolding of hurrying squirrels.

The fallow field sparkled as the early sun touched the jewelled spirals of the great spider webs, but there was not a spider to be seen, nor any to be heard dropping to the ground.

In the marsh, Kela stole like a white ghost toward the creek. Her tail was curled over her back, her eyes were shining, her black lips were open in a puckish grin. She was still well back from the edge when she sprang silently over the bank and dropped directly in front of a muskrat's doorway. Eagerly she looked up the creek, and down, and across the wide pool, but there was no outwitted muskrat swimming for escape. Her tail began to droop, her lips to close.

But after peering into the shadows under the overhang of the eastern bank, she held her banner at half mast and splashed noisily into the water, sending fingerlings flickering up the creek, across the shallows, and into another pool. Right on their tails she followed them, flushed out a larger school, and chased them to the next puddle.

Gaining and losing numbers of her finny flock, she continued the game until the creek widened over a bottom of fine, soft mud. Here she abandoned the fingerlings to seek out a resident swarm of tadpoles, but they, like the muskrat, were not there. Kela stared at the empty water, at the shadowless creek bed. No tadpoles. She gazed across the meadow, giving the tadpoles time to show up where they belonged. Still no tadpoles.

Her tail dropped. Her lips closed. She waded slowly up the creek, scanning the banks for frogs, watching for their wild leaps into the water. But this morning, no frogs.

Head down now, she proceeded up the creek, made an abrupt turn where a piece of the bank had just fallen away— and came face to face with a great snapping turtle.

Both Kela and the turtle stopped in their tracks. The turtle's head was up, Kela's down, and they stared at one another without blinking. Kela, I'm sure, outweighed the turtle by a good hundred pounds, but the turtle far outmatched her in armor and in viciousness. I stood watching them in dismay, not daring to give an order, fearful of that knife-sharp beak.

Moments went by. The creek water rippled about the two motionless animals. It curled over the edges of the turtle's shell and lapped at Kela's ankles.

More moments went by and Kela's tail rose in slow motion and curled easily over her back. Her lips opened in a smile. To my horror, she lowered her body, curving back on her hind legs, and she barked a friendly challenge to play. The turtle blinked his empty eyes but did not stir. Kela danced in the water and struck out with a playful paw. The turtle did not move.

Kela abruptly changed her tactics. She pulled herself to full height, raised her hackles, and barked down upon the intruder with full and angry authority. Again the turtle blinked, but stood without moving.

Kela cocked her head far to one side, her brow drawn, her dark eyes puzzled. What was this creature that ignored her challenges and defied her authority? She turned her head to the other side, studying the turtle, and then she looked up to me for orders, or advice.

And I failed her. I said nothing. Could this turtle be half-asleep, ready for hibernation? Was he being non-aggressive because he was partially in the water? Or was his faint reptilian brain boggled by the great white monster in his path?

That last I could not credit, for a snapping turtle fears nothing, has an irascible disposition and, on land at least, will snap at anything, living or dead, animal or vegetable. But this turtle was not even threatening. His rough brown carapace remained level; his long, saw-tooth tail trailed in the water; his pointed beak stayed tightly closed. He showed no intention either of lunging at Kela or turning from his path.

The next move was obviously up to Kela, and Kela decided to change partners. She leaped out upon the bank and raced about me in merry circles.

And the turtle? He did turn his head when Kela left the creek, but he dilly-dallied for only a moment. He ducked his head beneath the water, placed it against the bank, and, with one powerful forward lunge, drove his body into the soft earth where the bank-piece had broken away. Only the rear half of his shell and his long tail protruded into the water. A second powerful push with his rear legs and only his tail remained in sight. Now the soft earth heaved, the tail disappeared, and a mist of fine mud clouded the water. A bubble rose to the surface and broke. Another bubble rose. Broke. And all was still.

Buried Treasure

In the early summer the tree trimmers who cleared the right-of-way for the Gas and Electric Company left a great pile of wood chips at our woods edge for my use as a mulch.

Now, in November, I was belatedly trundling those chips, wheelbarrow load by wheelbarrow load, to the blueberry planting at the far end of the orchard. It was a slow job but a pleasant one, for the air was crisply clear and the sun shone brightly through the leafless trees onto the wood chips, the blueberries, and along the path between them, where goldenrod and purple asters, mowed off so many times, now flaunted their blossoms six inches above the ground.

Blue jays shrieked in the oak trees and a pair of red-tailed hawks screamed in the near distance above the brown meadow reeds. Beside me a white throat whistled absentmindedly, and the first flock of juncos flittered and twittered as it picked among the sassafras and the chinquapins.

Two crickets in faded black moved sluggishly along a sun-warmed stone and one of them produced a single rusty "Chir-rup," then lapsed into silence for the rest of the day.

The top layer of wood chips, possibly a foot thick, was well-weathered but dried out by wind and sunlight so that it was fluffy, light and easy to handle. Buried in this layer were dozens of pale, clean hickory nuts and polished brown acorns, neither of which had been ripe when the chips were piled there. Obviously I was disrupting the results of many squirrel-hours of work, and I placed the nuts and acorns in a heap as I found them, for I was certain they would be garnered again by the squirrel, or squirrels, to whom they belonged.

The squirrel who originally carries a nut in his teeth apparently impregnates it with his individual scent so that, months later, the squirrel can locate his own buried stores. Apparently, also, no squirrel will touch the food belonging to another, so if a squirrel is killed his stores remain where he left them, and it is these untouchable treasures more often than "forgotten" ones that result in the growth and spread of so many of our nut-bearing trees.

The scent these buried nuts carry must be of a penetrating quality—to a squirrel—for I have seen squirrels run over the crust of a foot of snow, suddenly stop, dig down in a flurry of flying crystals, and emerge with earth-stained nuts in their teeth.

Squirrels tend to concentrate the storing of their food in areas where the burying is easy, and by the time I had removed the light upper layer of wood chips I had collected half a peck of nuts and acorns. And a shovelful of snake eggs.

But the snake eggs were empty—hollow shells of dull creamy-white—each with a slit cut by an egg tooth before the baby snake emerged. The shells were nearly two inches long; thin, pliable, and almost shapeless in their emptiness; and the exterior surfaces were rough as though they had been sprinkled with a fine confetti of broken shells.

They were the eggs of a Blacksnake (Black Racer) and had been laid there soon after the chips were dropped. The ten- or twelve-inch, gray-blotched-with-brown baby snakes had probably uncoiled from those eggs by late August and were now somewhere in the woods asleep for the winter—those that had escaped the hungry searching of hawks, owls, cats, skunks and larger snakes, that is.

A covey of Bob Whites came strolling through the woods, their heads bobbing, their feet making a terrific racket in the dry leaves. Their leader, a white-faced male well out in front of his clustered followers, spied me working at the wood chips. His crest rose. He stretched his neck to its full length. He looked at me first with his left eye, then with his right, gave one single cry of alarm, and all eleven birds made an abrupt ninety-degree turn. They were not alarmed enough to take flight, but their straight little legs twinkled as they walked at a speed just beyond dignity into the shelter of a heap of limbs and branches placed there (by human agency) for just such emergencies.

Now I began to dig into the heavy, wet layer of chips where rain waters and ground dampness had penetrated but wind and sun had not, and with the first stroke of my shovel I partially decapitated a slender little ringneck snake. I don't know whether it went in there for food—a ringneck snake eats earthworms and small specimens of snakes, salamanders, lizards and frogs—or whether it went in to hibernate; but now it was dead.

It was about twelve inches long, its body was black, its underside yellow, and the narrow golden collar around its neck showed just a fleck of red. A pretty snake, a secretive snake, it is particularly fond of slipping under rotting wood, so the wood-chip pile was a natural hideaway for it.

But there was also food in there for a ringneck snake, for before the frosty sun went down on that November afternoon I had dug out four hibernating salamanders, little ones, scarcely three inches long, in plain shiny brown from head to tail and from top to bottom. Their eyes were closed, their bodies motionless; not even a twitch of a tail gave sign of life. They were deep in the torpor of hibernation.

I tucked the little salamanders into a small remnant of the wood chip pile, poured more chips over and around them, wished them a good winter's sleep, and wheeled my barrow away to its own shelter in the garage.

A Sharing of Persimmons

There are fifteen or twenty persimmon trees scattered across the hilly sweep of pasture land, most of them low and picturesquely grouped around outcroppings of gray, lichen-covered granite. In the spring their glossy, deep green leaves sparkle in the sunlight and obscure the small white blossoms that droop along the twigs and smaller branches. In the fall the long leathery leaves gleam a bright orange-red and hide the unripe fruits that hang from the same stiff calyces that held the springtime blossoms.

When the all-concealing leaves drop to the ground the nakedness of these trees is not quite complete, for each one clutches a multitude of orange-brown fruits in its multitude of twiggy fingers. And when winter's bitter weather arrives, each little fruit left still swinging in the wind is a flavorful bite of persimmon frappé.

And I love persimmon frappé. I love persimmons. Persimmons just ripe enough to be eaten. Persimmons soft and squashy and overripe. Persimmons cold and frosted with ice. Persimmons wrinkled and thawed and almost liquid with age.

Most persimmon trees carry their fruits high in their crowns, teasing and tantalizing, while their lower branches hang bare. But these trees load their lower branches just as prodigally as they fill their crowns, and I feast from October through December, and sometimes into the first months of the new year, with only an occasional leap to pull a higher branch down to picking level.

Each of my dogs, in succession, learned quickly the meaning of "Let's go get a persimmon!" At the sound of those words Kon-Tiki led off with a bound toward my favorite tree—to please me, I think, and because she, too, loved persimmons. Kela goes more slowly, but goes to please me, I hope, and because she knows we won't go anywhere else until we've visited the hill pasture. She does not like persimmons.

So Kela makes no inroads on the persimmon crop and only once or twice in half a dozen years, to my knowledge, has another human being picked any of the luscious fruit; but the crop is not left entirely, nor even mostly, to me.

There is a battle-happy mockingbird who tries to control all twenty trees, and he flies himself ragged in his efforts to drive winged poachers from his far-flung domain. He does an astoundingly good job of it, too, probably because the area is so open and because most birds would rather fly than fight.

I saw him outwitted, though, one December day, by a flock of fifteen cedar waxwings who, after being chased from one tree to another for almost an hour, simply split into three small groups, flew low over the snow-covered ground, and came up into the trees undetected.

Once they started to rip open his precious fruits, the mockingbird saw them and pounced upon them, but he could only harass one small group at a time, and all the cedar waxwings managed to stuff themselves with persimmons.

The mockingbird was outnumbered, and the waxwings were tricky, but I think the weather had a lot to do with his defeat. It was a bitter winter day, darkly clouded, and gusting winds kept lifting the surface snow into the air in shifting curtains or in stinging blasts, creating confusion and cutting visibility. Whatever their advantages, the vagabonding waxwings were gone the next morning and the mockingbird went back to his easier task of keeping off starlings, blue jays and rival mockers.

Persimmons on the tree are food for the birds, and fallen ones are quickly scooped up by the resident foxes, skunks, raccoons and opossums. There are hollow trees complete with raccoons in the nearby woods, a lived-in fox den among the rocks in the ravine, and at least three groundhog holes right there in the pasture.

From the fox den to the persimmon trees I find only fox tracks; but from the groundhog holes the star-shaped tracks of opossums and the dainty toed-in prints of skunks make single-minded pathways directly to the trees—and wide-wandering, notional meanderings on the return trip to warmth and darkness.

Raccoons come from the woods most often, but sometimes I find the track of a raccoon mingled with the others on the pathways between the persimmon trees and the groundhog holes, and then I know that yet another spare bedspace in groundhog lodgings is occupied by a needy sojourner. The groundhog is sound asleep in his own sealed-off bedchamber and he does not know and does not care who takes refuge in his outer burrow.

I have never seen a raccoon eating a persimmon, although I know they do, but once I did find one up the tree. Or perhaps he found me. It was early in the morning of another December day, not stormy, but cold and clear, with an inch of new snow on the ground, all soft and fluffy and marked with the mingled tracks of neighborhood animals. I did not realize that more tracks led to the tree than led away from it.

With the tree at my back and Kela at my side I stood tiptoe and plucked a frozen persimmon from an outer branch. I bit through thin tissue skin into sweet icy pulp, closed my eyes to savor its frosty flavor, and felt the force of staring eyes on the back of my neck. I looked uneasily over my shoulder but saw no one. Kela was undisturbed, so I went back to my eating.

The feeling of being watched continued and, though Kela remained perfectly calm, I grew increasingly uneasy and finally turned around so that I faced the direction from which the staring seemed to come. But still I saw no one.

Something made me look into the tree and there was a young raccoon about six feet above me. He was leaning against the trunk and surveying me steadily, with bright and curious eyes, through his dark burglar's mask.

Persimmons and opossums go together just as naturally as love and marriage are supposed to, so quite often I find an opossum or two perched in one of the trees. Whether they are ignoring Kela and me or whether their primitive little brains just do not register our presence I have never been able to decide, but they go on with their eating as though we did not exist, and I am glad that it is so. To watch, and to hear, an opossum eating a persimmon is a vicarious experience in the absolutely uninhibited joy of eating.

The opossum perches himself comfortably somewhere in the crown of the tree in easy reaching distance of several persimmons. He clings to the branches with his bare pink feet and hooks his hairless gray tail over the limb behind him for balance. Then he dreamily closes his eyelids over his round dark eyes, and, with the fifty teeth in his shallow jaws, he chops one delectable fruit after another in a lip-smacking, saliva-spattering, juice-slobbering ecstasy.

A Winter's Tale of Woodpeckers

Woodpeckers, whether in woods, cornfields, or clumps of weedy growths, seem to typify the very depths of darkest winter. Yet, with the probable exception of the yellow-bellied sapsucker which I rarely see, all the members of the woodpecker tribe who winter with us are with us the whole year through. They feed and court and rear their young well hidden by the covering greens of the leafy seasons, but when the woods next to the house stands bare, their foraging over the rough bark of the trees is visible to any watcher indoors or out. And every winter storm brings more of these crisp-uniformed individuals dodging in from tree to tree to eat at our feeding stations under the lilacs and along the edge of the woods.

The flickers are the first to come in. But then the flickers are always here, perfectly at home the year around, accepting, now, the fortuitous appearance of sunflower seeds and cracked corn as their natural and divine right. I suspect that the survival kit of these flickers (and all our winter birds) includes the knowledge that lilac bushes shed sunflower seeds and cracked corn during the winter months. Through all their lives it has been so. They nest each spring in the white oak stub just inside the woods where their parents nested before them. They drink from the crockery-patched-with-concrete bird bath beside the lilacs all summer long, dust themselves in the bare earth beneath the bushes, and expect—this mustachioed male and his clear-faced mate—to find winter sustenance there.

But the downy woodpeckers never eat together. This white-backed little fellow never shares a place at table with the creature who happens, through a quirk of nature, to be his mate. They seem never to be far apart, winter or summer, rearing their young, looking out for themselves, keeping in touch by a constantly repeated, flat-toned "pick"; but she dares not approach the feeding station when he is there, or, if she arrives first, he sends her away before settling down himself.

Neither of them is much afraid of me, and, as winter storms worsen, they watch from some woodland covert until I come out to replenish the food, then flit from tree trunk to tree trunk, zigzagging closer and closer, until one or the other lands nearly at my feet to snatch cracked corn from the snowy ground. The little male reminds me of an Indian warrior with that one red feather tucked into his back hair, and the female, of course, is his strong-minded but judiciously retiring squaw.

A larger warrior, dressed in practically identical checkered and spotted black and white, and with one large red feather tucked into the back of his hair, came dodging through the trees one snowy, blowing day. He backed down the trunk of a hickory tree and fell to work with gusto cracking the shells of the sun-flower seeds scattered at its base. This brave looked twice the size of the male downy a few feet away, and the downy's bill appeared hopelessly dainty in comparison with the heavy tool the newcomer was using. Identical dress, larger size, formidable bill—I knew I was looking at the only hairy woodpecker I had ever seen.

Was he only passing through? Would the plentiful spread of winter food entice him to settle here? A sudden blast of wind swirled the snow into a whirling curtain that veiled and covered the feeding birds. The hairy woodpecker took off into the face of it, beat his way across the open lawn, crashed headlong into the glass of the kitchen window, and broke his sturdy neck.

The zebra-backed, silky-red-helmeted, faintly-pink-bellied birds who are inexcusably called red-bellied woodpeckers are as prevalent and as noisy as flickers. They nest in hollows in limbs and trees high above the ground in what I am pleased to call my territory and I meet with them everywhere on my year-around walks. They come early and late to the winter feeding stations with the single-minded purpose of eating sunflower seeds. They crack the shells and extract the kernels right there on the ground, swiftly, efficiently. They battle the bluejays and other members of their own clan indiscriminately, and they fill the air with loud, twanging "chips" and hostile-sounding "churrs."

And I look in vain for the red-headed woodpeckers once so

plentiful among the oak limbs in the woods and backyards of the countryside.

The woodpecker tribe is a diversely colored and diversely patterned lot, but there is an essential woodpeckeriness about them—not due entirely to the stout, stubby legs or to the two toes forward and two toes back or to the stiff-feathered tails propped downward against the tree—that tells the initiate "this is a woodpecker" even if he has never seen this particular species before.

One dark, cold January day, Kela and I walked across the hilltop toward a small grove of sassafras trees. We were scarcely fifty feet from its northern edge when a black-and-white bird the size of a crow came through the trees from the east and landed fifteen or twenty feet up on a dead tree right in front of us. The bird was mostly black, some white on its neck and head; the head was beautifully, bountifully crested, but the crest on the head was black. I stood with my hand buried in Kela's mane and forced my eyes to see some red on that woodpecker's head. But there was none.

The bird hopped two steps up the tree with its tail propped sturdily against the trunk, then backed two steps down. He hopped several steps to the right and peered behind the tree, then twice that many hops to the left and peered behind from that side. Center front again, and, without so much as a glance at us, he spread his wings and flew away in the direction from which he came. If he exposed white markings on his wings as he flew away I do not remember them—I was still trying to color him red.

I never saw that bird again and I do not know what he was. He just could not have been an ivory bill, near extinction down there on the Singer Tract in northern Louisiana, although the female looks like that; and if the young pileated woodpecker shows no red the several books I've consulted have failed to tell me so.

What that black-crested bird had to do with it, I do not know, but within the week a winter wind took the top out of that dead tree. Broke it off exactly on the line marked by the four-toed feet of the black woodpecker as he hopped to right and to left and peered around the trunk.

February: Month of Skunk Romance

 rom the graying twilight of evening until the gray half-
light of dawning, there is something amiss with a February night
if the odor of skunk musk does not hang pervasively on the air.
February is mating time for the striped skunks of our area, and
only wildly bitter weather will keep them confined to winter
shelter when nature insists upon romance.

Skunks do not hibernate as groundhogs do; that is, they
never, or rarely, sink into the torpor of actual hibernation, but
they do den up—in groundhog holes, under buildings, in old
barns—to sleep through blizzards, gales and deluges.

Male skunks are solitary even when sheltering from winter
storms, but females roll up, warm and snug, half a dozen or
more together, in the darkness of their winter hidey-holes,
thereby multiplying both their bodily comfort and their chances
for coming safely through the dangerous times.

Only violent weather qualifies as dangerous in February, so
that merely snowy or merely rainy weather finds the entire
skunk population on the prowl. The females trail their "Follow
Me" perfume wherever they wander and the males urgently
seek those scented paths, and do wild and musky battle with
others of their sex who search the same territory.

Actually, skunks are neither smelly nor hostile; they simply
live by the precept of don't-bother-me-and-I'll-not-bother-you.
Their musk is so concentrated that although they spray only the
equivalent of two or three liquid drops, it is a formidable
weapon against any creature close enough to receive its full
force. Its sulphide odor can be smelled for half a mile.

That same odor, sprayed but faintly, is the fragrance used
by the female skunk to enthrall her clumsy, pursuing male. She
shrugs off his first inept advances and, while he stamps and
patters and grunts about, she arches her back, raises her long
and plumy tail, and wafts the tiniest bit of magical perfume

onto the frosty air. The male is lifted on the wings of love, captures the maiden trembling before him, and subdues her on the spot.

Nature is frugal. All her inventions have multiple uses. The same magical perfume, possessed by both male and female skunks, is both an alluring love potion and an overwhelming weapon allowing all skunks to walk in the fearlessness of ever-ready defenses, which, let it be added, they use only upon provocation.

The difficulty is, of course, to know what will provoke a particular skunk. The theory is that only surpise, abrupt movement and outright attack will do so; their small, dark eyes provide them with such a poor view of what is going on about them that it is possible, with quiet carefulness, to approach quite closely even a full-grown skunk in the freedom of his hunting territory.

Once upon a time I put this theory to the perilous test— and won.

The rain had fallen gently all that February night, and in the morning, when only the faintest light glowed above the hills, a mist arose from the cold earth, curtaining off the low valleys, creeping over the rises, hiding the woods, and finally sweeping across orchard, garden, lawn, and house to leave me standing outside the kitchen door in a drizzly, gray-white cloud.

In the cottony silence I heard not the slightest rustle of leaves, not the slightest swishing of grasses, but out of the woods and across the lawn a large, striped skunk came mincing on dainty, toed-in feet. Its face was almost entirely white, and this whiteness extended back over its head in a solid cap, then divided to pass down each side in a broad stripe that extended the entire length of its tail, and ended there in a plumy white tip.

Head down and tail down it moved in various loops and semicircles through the short grasses of the dooryard with its pointed black nose skimming just a hair's breadth above the wet earth. It paused. Little black hands dug swiftly at the base of a grass clump and sharp white teeth made an end to the fat grub he unearthed. He walked right by me without the slightest acknowledgment that I was there and dug into a mole-run at the edge of the flagstones.

This skunk, I decided, was either exceedingly deficient in all his senses, or he knew and trusted me from a long association of which I was mostly unaware, or he had a quite sure and abiding faith in the efficacy of his own defenses.

With a swift and effortless motion of his head, the skunk pulled a long-tailed mouse from a matting of thyme. I realized that, whatever his reasons for ignoring me, his senses were well-enough attuned for some highly intensive food gathering. Furthermore, he was both calm and well-tempered, even though it was the middle of the mating season. I would never have a better opportunity to try a close approach.

Accordingly, when the skunk had consumed the mouse and resumed his hunting I put myself into silent-as-possible motion and walked warily, somewhat tensely, ten or a dozen feet away from him. But since I knew he could fire in any direction from his extrusible scent glands and that I could, at that distance, not possibly escape a gassing if he became annoyed, I decided to trust him. Relaxing, I walked at his side, only four or five feet away, and the two of us strolled the length of the yard in the dark gray drizzle.

But now my small companion re-entered the woods where dark tree trunks came between us, and dripping low growth hid him, now and then, from my sight. I became increasingly concerned that I might come around a tree and surprise him, or stumble upon him in the undergrowth, or alarm him by tripping over a fallen limb; so I stood beside the gum tree just inside the woods, watched him patter off without me, and discreetly returned to the house.

The Search for Spring

Cold and bright and thirty-one days long, March holds the turning of the year in the folds of its weeks and, most often, buffets us with winter more than it laves us in spring.

Nature manages, all the year long, to appear undependable, capricious, whimsical, even mad; but never quite so outrageously so as in this third wild month when the violet blossoming on the sunny bank is likely to have its blue eye filled with snow, and the groundhog nibbling sweet new clover in the lee of the gray stones will most surely be driven back into his burrow by raw and biting winds.

March winds have to blow, I'm told. It is one of the few things you can depend upon about March. Masses of cold air have accumulated in the arctic regions while the sun has been off in the south increasing the heat of the shimmering tropics. Strong currents, now, are flowing south from the cold regions, and other currents equally strong are flowing north from the warm ones, and when the two systems collide, or play leap-frog, the proverbial winds of March result.

Wild winds they are, and mad winds, but they help to dry the earth left oozing and soggy by winter; they play a tremendous part in the vital turning-over of the waters in lakes and ponds, and they stimulate the circulation of life juices in trees and lesser plants.

Those trees and lesser plants know another dependable thing about March: its sunlight. Not that today will be sunny— or that it won't—but that the sun is there, above the horizon, just a little longer on each successive day. The sun and its heat and light are irresistible. The snow has to go, the ice has to melt, the earth has to warm, eggs have to hatch, and roots have to stretch and grow.

Each life was shut down for the winter with its own special

code for awakening in the spring, and the key that triggers the opening mechanism is the sun's light and warmth. Insects, both eggs and over-wintering adults, are quickly warmed, and so are the surface rootings of quick-growing plants; but it takes a little longer for warmth to reach the turtle, the earthworm and the frog.

And that is another amazing thing about chaotic March— its ultimate orderliness. Whether spring comes on in a long, slow curve, or whether it arrives with a warm wind and a hot sun all in one week, everything happens in its own time. Nothing gets out of its place in line.

The robin does not arrive in any numbers before the earthworms unthread themselves from the tangles in their dark cellars. The first butterflies that drift about the woodlands drink tree sap and are not dependent upon the nectar of flowers yet to bloom. And many a flying insect is livening up the marshes before the first frogs arise from the mud.

It is the old food chain again, and the first to arrive is he who gets eaten—the tiniest, the least able to fight back. And that is why I begin, sometime during the first week of March, to bring back from each morning's walk a dropper of water taken from the warming shallows of the pond or from a sunny puddle in the marsh. Under the lens of a microscope, in the amazing world of the water drop, on a certain morning I shall see some unbelievable creature moving about. He will be seeking, of course, his own tinier food and at the same time inadvertently offering himself upon the table of the next higher order —some tiny crustacean, or the larval form of an insect.

I am never quite sure that the first animalcule I find was not warmed out of his encystment in my pocket or, for that matter, on the glass slide itself; but if, in the next day or so, his numbers and kinds increase then I can say to myself, "Well, spring is here." But I say it under my breath, for there is a tremendous discontinuity between the world of winter-bound humanity and the one under the lens. However, now I can walk through the wet places knowing that the life I sense with all my being is truly stirring there.

Then comes a day when I find small flies and tiny gnats busy about the fleshy flowerheads in the twisted spathes of skunk cabbage, and the catkins hanging loose and free on the alder bushes by the stream. I nod my head. "Spring is here." But still I say it softly.

And one morning, in a sunny curve of the stream bank where the water flows quietly, I shall find half a dozen water striders standing about on the surface of the water looking dazed and newly arrived and not knowing what to do about it. Every now and then two or three will drift together, then solemnly disentangle their long legs and stand about as before. And I shall make up for their apparent lack of joyousness by smiling broadly, for I love water striders (and privately call them minnie skippers), and I shall say aloud, but still to myself, "Well, spring is really here."

And then comes an afternoon when the sun lies warm and bright like a golden veil across the meadow and the marshes. A tiny sleighbell tinkles. Another sleigh bell rings. And suddenly the once-winter world is filled with the wildly tintinabulating chorus of the spring peepers as they gather for their primeval rites, and I say joyously, and aloud, and to everyone I meet, "Spring is here! The peepers are back!" And everyone with half an ear responds, "I know!"

Spring Passage

Except as high and usually noisy wedges moving across the equinoctial skies, migrating water birds are not much a part of my out-of-door world. Their main flyways lie well to the east of my home, and it is only the flocks off-course, or the adventuresome flocks exploring back roads, whose flights I see.

There are enough of these eccentrics, though, so that I always know when the Canada geese are leaving the bay, or returning to it; for their honking, dog-barking voices override all other country sounds as their dark skeins sweep over, every bird seeming to jockey for place, argue the route, or generally cause a commotion in the flock.

Ducks I almost never see, and snow geese I saw but once— a silent skein of round, white bodies balanced between wing-tips enamel black, high against the blue of a bright March sky, and never forgotten.

And swans. Whistling swans. Those great, graceful, snow-white birds whose long necks point their black bills to the far horizon like compass needles to be followed without fear or deviation; those splendid birds whose northward flights fill me with a yearning excitement I can scarcely contain and cannot explain, even to myself—those birds I have seen only several times in a dozen years. And I remember every flight.

One springtime morning, Kela and I walked along the ridge of the pasture hills, soft grass and soft earth beneath our feet, the air filled with the o-kra-leeing of redwings from the marshes, and a wedge of whistling swans flying from the south with the light of the rising sun on their snow-feathered bodies.

They were flying so low that I could see the black bills tipping the lines of outstretched necks, the dark feet tucked up against arcs of spread white tails, almost feel the lift and the pull of every curving wing. Twenty-five birds formed a perfect wedge, twelve birds to each side, and their leader making the point.

They flew in trim formation without the usual full-toned clamor of swan voices. Only their leader, at the apex of their flight, fluted a constant musical note. The others seemed content with desultory, though far-carrying, comments among closest neighbors.

A flock of seasoned birds, I assumed, all well known to one another, and settled down, now, from the excitement and confusion of take-off, for a long and steady pull to the north. Flying in confidence and purpose, headed for the coasts and islands of the Arctic seas where a month, six weeks, from now each mated pair will find a nesting site on the borders of a marsh and set about their building with reeds and grasses and cushions of moss.

The female will warm the half-dozen white eggs for the five or so weeks necessary to develop and hatch the down-covered cygnets; but the male will feed her and stand guard over her and over their nest.

For swans are truly family birds. Both male and female will feed and train their little ones, and the cygnets will run with equal assurance to father or to mother, often climbing upon their backs and riding in safety between partially uplifted parental wings.

But those parental wings cannot lift them into the air, for the parent birds moult all their flight feathers at this time, and no one in the family can fly. By the time new flight feathers grow in, the cygnets will also be well-feathered, and they will all take to the air together. They strengthen their wing muscles and learn to fly in proper wedge formation so that when autumn comes to the northland, they can join forces with other local families and all fly south together.

The family stays pretty much together through the first winter in the south, but when the restlessness of northerly migration-time stirs through the flocks, the cygnets leave their parents and take off with their peers on adventures of their own.

But the parent birds never separate. They mate in their first or second year, and live in unquestioned faithfulness for the span of their indissolubly mated lives. And forever after. For swans of a mated pair are strictly monogamous. Not slightly so, or partially so, but completely so. This is a situation neither moral nor rigorous, but simply the-way-things-are. When one dies, even in the first year of mating, the other goes on alone to the end of his life, though that time stretch on for years.

These thoughts took a flash of time to think—though minutes to tell—and while I planned the season ahead for these swans, the flock drew abreast of us, flying above the farm pond that silvered the foot of the hill where we stood.

At this exact moment, the bird at the end of the western leg of the wedge uttered a strange, ringing cry that sent surprising chills of apprehension rippling over my body. He left his place in line and flew steadily up its outer edge, passing so closely to his fellows that their beating wingtips nearly touched. He crossed the path of the formation leader and swung down the eastern leg of the V so that he looked each of these flyers in the face as he passed. When he reached the last bird in line, his voice rang again in a cry of such utter desolation that, without conscious translation on my part, pain twisted in the pit of my stomach.

The swan turned about, sped swiftly up the eastern leg, crossed again in front of the leader, and flew down the western leg, looking, now, into the faces of these.

When he came to the end of the line he did not call again, nor pause, but flew straight on, without a falter, back the way they had come. While the unruffled flock pulled steadily northward, one lone white figure beat its way to the south against the immense blue of the sky.

Three days later, a whistling swan, flying from the south, came gliding down to float gracefully on the rippling surface of the farm pond where never a swan had floated before. There was nothing to distinguish this swan from any other of his kind, yet I knew, illogically, that it was the same bird I had seen desert his northward flight above this very pond, days before.

I watched him as I could through the following days while he floated in silence on the center of the pond. He did not eat. He did not move, except as the current moved him. He sat on the water craning his neck and scanning the skies hour after hour after hour.

Late in the afternoon of his fifth day on the pond, with a gray haze obscuring the horizon hills and a thunderstorm grumbling in the south, the lone swan lifted himself from the pond and headed into the north. His white wings beat the heavy air as he strained for altitude. His single cry rang down the misted valley and careened between the hills. It echoes there still.

The First Day of the Tent Caterpillar

Yesterday only the faintest pulse of life was discernible in the brown band of eggs that encircles the tip of a low wild-cherry branch. This morning's sunlight is working its April magic and I can see, in each tiny egg, a baby tent caterpillar attempting to cut his way through the transparent shell.

The first one pokes his head through the hole he has cut and his thin little body follows. He stretches himself up and down, to left and to right, and then tries out his six pairs of wobbly legs. He is less than an eighth of an inch long and through my magnifying glass his dark little face looks kittenish and new.

But no kitten ever moved out upon his life with such solemn instinct as this caterpillar and half a dozen of his brothers and sisters who struggle out of their shells as I watch. Head to tail, all in a line, they walk away from their empty eggs, down the twig and down the branch; spinning out gossamer threads as they go, laying down a path for their later-hatching siblings to follow.

Every few steps each one touches his head to the branch at his feet and attaches the thread firmly to the bark. Here one wobbles a little out of line to the left and there a little out of line to the right, and all the time other little caterpillars keep hatching out of eggs and following down the twig and spinning gossamer threads of their own. The shiny path becomes thicker and wider with every passing caterpillar.

The caterpillar leading the march bumps into a twig and he stops to explore. He finds three small branches growing up like tent poles in reverse, so he sets about to build a tent upon them.

All the caterpillars, and by now there are quite a few of them, begin to mill about and to crawl over the bases of these little branches. It is only when I single out one caterpillar to watch that I can see what they all are doing.

This particular caterpillar crawls an inch up one forking branch, puts his head down to attach a thread, then crawls back down to the main branch and up the next fork for the same distance. Here he puts his head down again and I see that he has actually stretched a line in the air between the two branches. The line is loose and wet and dark but as it dries it stretches tightly between the two tent poles. It turns white as it dries and it glistens in the sunlight and twinkles in the faintly stirring breeze.

Over and over again the caterpillar stretches his lines. Over and over again all of his siblings keep doing the same. Soon there are so many lines in the same places that they form cables. And soon there are so many cables that the caterpillars begin to crawl out upon them and to work across them so that they are actually weaving a lattice-work between the tent poles.

All this time others have been straggling down the gossamer highway, and as soon as each one arrives he sets to work, not going through the whole process, but starting in at whatever stage the work has reached.

When all the eggs have hatched, there are nearly two hundred minute caterpillars crawling over the tent, crossing and criss-crossing their silken lines until the tent covering is a filmy, silver-white fabric, beautiful, but with hundreds upon hundreds of tiny holes gaping between the threads.

This activity goes on so long that I begin to think guiltily of duties unattended, when suddenly all the little caterpillars crawl to the top of the tent and pack themselves together in a long row side by side. They lie so still that I think they are resting, but, through the lens, I see their tiny heads moving back and forth, back and forth, rhythmically and together.

I squint through the glass and pull it back for greatest magnification until I can see that those little creatures are attaching dark and sticky loops to the dry white fabric. They are filling in the holes in their tent! I watch, enchanted. When they complete that section they all move together to a fresh spot and again the little heads tick back and forth like minute pendulums and more holes are filled in.

It is almost noon when the little caterpillars creep off their rain-tight roof and crowd through the round doorway they have left in the underside of their tent. They lie side by side on the white floor and the gleaming roof stretches scarcely an inch above their heads. The tent they have built is tiny, but it is airy and spacious for such newly-hatched tent-makers.

While the caterpillars rest I dust out my own shelter, but I keep running in and out lest I miss the next episode in the new lives. It is nearly four o'clock when the caterpillars, one behind the other, creep through their doorway and march out upon a branch. Each one lays down a thread of silk as he goes, making a pathway all can follow safely back to the family tent.

The whole brood crowds onto the first April-sized leaf they come to, and they begin to chew out the tender parts between the veins as industriously as they filled in the holes between the threads of their tent.

They stuff themselves until their sides bulge and then, one after the other, they trail back to the tent to rest and to grow until tomorrow afternoon when they will stuff themselves again.

Tent caterpillars grow very fast when there are plenty of leaves and the weather stays sunny—they don't eat when it is raining—so they quickly outgrow their first tiny tent and build another around it. When the second tent becomes too crowded they will build a third one around it, and even, perhaps, a fourth.

One year I gently pulled apart the largest tent I had ever seen. I found seven tents, each one completely surrounding all the previous ones and each roof scarcely an inch above the next.

The Woodchicks

On a warm May morning when the sunlight shimmered the dew on the grasses, Kela and I splashed up a pebble-bottomed creek between blackberry patches that made land travel uncomfortable there, and climbed the sloping clay banks where clumps of daylilies replaced the slashing briers.

The low-lying, triangular piece of flat-land we now crossed was not wet enough to be called a marsh, yet it was definitely not farming ground. In September it would be golden and purple with Joe Pye weed, tick sunflowers and goldenrod, but now it was a mass of May greenery through which we waded to our knees.

Where the land began to rise we breathed the earthy smell of wet brown leaves crushed beneath our feet, while we walked under the fresh new leafings of box elder and swamp maple trees.

And just there, where the warming sunlight filtered through, making a flicker of light and shadow, a woodcock hen went up from so close to Kela's feet that she must have stepped on its tailfeathers.

Kela and I, startled, stopped in our tracks. The bird flew across in front of us, rising scarcely four feet above the ground, and dropped over a low fence draped in honeysuckle vines, not twenty feet away.

The flight took only seconds, but the picture of it was etched on my mind. There was something strange about it. We had a profile of a woodcock in flight instead of the back-and-tail angle we were accustomed to, and the bird was so close we could have caught it had we not been so stilled by surprise.

But something about the flight puzzled me. It was the angle of the bird's body, I decided. She had held her body almost perpendicular to the ground—in level flight—and had curved her stubby tail downward, holding it beneath her, against the backs of her legs. Her long bill was pressed tightly down against her breast, as though she were straining upward with her neck muscles.

She seemed to fly heavily, too, and something about her legs looked unusual. As though she were carrying something between her feathered thighs, I thought—and a light flicked on in my brain. She must have been carrying a baby woodcock away from danger (us) to safe hiding behind the fence. I had read about woodcocks transporting their chicks that way, but never before had I seen it happen. And one baby woodcock whisked away meant other baby woodcocks were somewhere close by.

Neither Kela nor I had stirred. I ordered Kela to "wait a minute" (our equivalent for "stay"), and, without moving my own feet, began to scrutinize the ground. At first all I could discern was brown leaves and flickering sunlight; but gradually three tiny woodcock chicks took shape beside Kela's right front foot, so close that several long hairs of her ankle lay across the nearest chick.

The brown and buffy three sat flat upon the ground, snuggled like sleepy chicks in a nest, but their dark, liquid eyes were wide open, staring into unknown dangers. But not the flick of an eyelid betrayed them. Downy as ducklings, their shining brown bills as long as their bodies, they must have been only hours, possibly only minutes, out of the nest; yet, in in-stinctive obedience to their mother's warning, they sat like porcelain figures, seeming not even to breathe.

I had never seen any but adult woodcocks before—and those only on the wing or pulling earthworms from the mud at a considerable distance from me—so I was fascinated by these miniatures close enough to touch and quiet enough to observe. I looked for their ears in front of their high-placed eyes and studied their rounded bills with the flexible tips that would be such prodigious takers of earthworms some few weeks from now.

The naturalist in me wanted hours to study, to take notes, to pick up a woodchick and closely examine it. The coward in me was fearful of Kela's swallowing the chicks should she discover them. The soft-headed human being in me was rueful of the fright we had already given the mother and her brood and of the terror we were even now prolonging for them.

The naturalist lost, and I think I am sorry. But Kela began to sniff about curiously, lowering her nose toward the ground. I quickly eased her away, coming between her and the woodchicks. As I did, I stepped on a dead branch which snapped beneath my foot. One end of it, four or five inches long, flipped into the air and dropped across the soft-skinned bill of one of the chicks. The chick did not move. Not a muscle trembled. Not an eyelid flickered. I looked upon them with wonder and with yearning—and led my big white friend away.

We climbed the rise until we were screened from the birds by pines and honeysuckle, and there we stopped. I found a thin veil in the screening where I could peer down upon the chicks and where, hopefully, the woodhen could not see me, and prepared myself for a wait, hoping to see the hen collect her young.

Kela, usually so impatient of any pauses in our walks unless she decrees them, sat for a while on her haunches looking at me with questioning eyes. Then she gave up, stretched out at my feet and went to sleep, and, thankfully, did not snore.

I stayed as close to motionless as I could, shamed by those infant birds; but I flicked my eyelids now and again, moved my chest in shallowest breathing, and shifted muscles here and there as the minutes went by.

The myriad noises of a bright May morning went on about us. Killdeer cried and meadowlarks sang and redwings o-kraleed; mosquitoes whined and honey bees hummed and blue flies buzzed in the sunlight.

And then, lower than the other noises, but clearly and distinctly, a soft chirring sound came from the vine-draped fence. Instantly, the three chicks skittered across the brown leaves to disappear into the honeysuckle and, without doubt, into comforting shelter under the woodhen's wings.

All on a Bright June Morning

arly in the day, before dawn, I stepped outside my door into a world shadowy, silent, and waiting. A chipping sparrow in the mockorange bush tested the morning with a tentative buzz. He listened, and I listened, but no bird answered his call.

The dark sky turned to silver, and the chipping sparrow sent another call, a pebbled buzz, into the paling air. Only deeper silence answered him, and both of us waited and listened.

Then from the east, from the hills, woods and marshes hidden from me by my own rising woodland, came a tide of birdsong. It rolled toward me, sweetly cacophonous, until it engulfed my own small woods where, all together, a vireo sang, a phoebe called, and a woodthrush fluted; the chipping sparrow buzzed, and a song sparrow sang; a blue jay screamed, a pheasant cock crowed, a cardinal whistled, and all the robins in the orchard added their voices in rollicking welcome to the day.

With the concert swelling and the morning brightening fast, Kela and I slipped through the blossoming chinquapins into the mysterious, green-lighted world of the woods.

Under the crescendo of song we walked almost in silence; our legs brushing through low forests of May apple umbrellas made the only sound of our passing. A scattering of late rue anemone starred the dim woods floor. False Solomon's seal opened clusters of tiny white flowers, and striped wintergreen held pink petals tightly bound in buds. Under the oak trees the otherworldly whiteness of the earliest Indian pipes tipped through layers of dead brown leaves.

Still in the shadows of high-crowned trees, we waded the stony creek and climbed its far bank, but at the top of the hill we came out under a coppery sky into an open field of red clover, ox-eye daisies, fleabane and yarrow. The first black-eyed Susans were blossoming, and Queen Anne's lace, and blue chicory, and moth mullein with its tilted blossoms poised on their toes.

As we stood watching the color changes in the sky the almost-summer sun topped the eastern hills. It was a morning without dew, and so almost at once a host of butterflies were fluttering about us—cabbages and sulphurs swarming over the clover, monarchs and swallowtails dipping across the field, admirals and fritillaries in swifter, stronger flight, and dark mourning cloaks floating along the edges of the woods.

I picked a handful of wild strawberries and one ripe black raspberry and ate them while Kela investigated a groundhog hole under a tangle of fragrant honeysuckle.

We turned and entered our neighbor's pastures at their highest hilltop boundary. We walked through waist-high grasses with the blossoming timothy puffing clouds of pollen into the air with our every step. With every footstep, too, we sent dozens of gnats and small, pale moths into the air to be gobbled quickly by barn swallows darting and wheeling just over our heads. Kela snapped at a low-circling swallow and the whole flock swept ever lower, apparently for the pure sport of dodging her jaws.

From the hillside above the pond we watched a muskrat swim across the water and disappear under the bank. A kingfisher dived from the limb of a dead oak beside the pond and rose from the water with a flash of silver twisting in his bill. With his crest up, his wings streaming water, he lifted himself to a willow below the dam to devour his slippery catch.

Fish were rising all over the pond, and, in the shallows, small fry and tadpoles scooted into deeper water as we passed. A greenish mass of frog eggs a foot or more across hung in the surface algae near the shore. Whirligig beetles spun like senseless mechanical toys on the water's surface. Clear-winged dragonflies darted above the pond collecting insects in the baskets formed by their six hairy legs, and damsel flies in glinting greens and blues rested with folded wings on the grasses overhanging the water.

Down through the marsh we walked, sinking to our ankles in the ooze, and brushing by blossoming reeds, and penstemon, and marsh violets. Ignoring the scolding redwings above us, we watched for tree frogs in the reed clumps and for green frogs and bull frogs leaping into concealment.

On the bank above the creek our feet crushed the sweet vernal grass and filled the air about us with an elusive fragrance. A cottontail rabbit bounced down the bank and a garter snake slithered into the grasses.

Once again we waded the creek and entered the sunlight and shadows of our own woods. Chipmunks squeaked and darted into stone piles. Gray squirrels flirted their tails, climbed halfway up tree trunks and stopped to scold.

A red fox, crouching low, slipped through the May apples and we were off on a chase. Running, leaping, zigzagging, around the woods we went. Across the clearing and down to the creek. Into the creek and up its mossy stones for a hundred feet—and we lost the trail. We quartered and we searched. Off we went again. Into a neighbor's woods, up its hills and down its dales; into another neighbor's pasture and back into our own woods again on the run.

But the temperature of the June day had reached summer strength and Kela was tiring. Abruptly, she lost interest in the hunt and, head down, plodded homeward.

I glanced ahead, into the dim light under the trees, and there sat the fox. Casually. On his haunches. Not fifteen feet from our path. His eyes were on Kela, not frightened, not even wary, just interested. Not once did he lift his eyes to me. He watched Kela as we drew abreast of him. Watched Kela as we ambled past. Watched Kela until we were fifty feet away. Then he got to his feet, yawned broadly, and trotted off through the woods.

A Battle-Happy Butterfly

It was a poet's summer day. The air was dry. The sun was bright, and puffs of cloud drifted across a sky of tingling blue.

With trowel in hand, I approached a weedy border and noted, on passing the hostas, that a small brown butterfly was perched atop the tallest spike. The tips of his wings were pressed together above his back, and his head and thorax looked broad and bulky beneath them. "Skipper," I thought as I went by, and I knelt to my weeding.

Honey bees were humming in the snowy edging of sweet alyssum and one of them, filled with nectar, rose into the air, bound for the hive. She swung in an arc toward the hostas and when she was still ten feet away the butterfly launched himself from his lavender tower, pounced upon her back, and sent her careening off into the distance.

Darting and dashing in every direction the Skipper chased a fly, a wasp, a day-flying moth, and thoroughly cleared the area before he returned to his observation post.

A battling butterfly! Would he attack me? I dropped a handful of purslane into a trash bag and went to find out. The butterfly turned to face me as I came. I bent toward him until my face was only inches from his, and he looked me in the eye and he did not move.

I returned his mirthless stare, looking him over for identification purposes. He was a skipper, all right, but which skipper?

He was brown, all brown—eyes, head, body, legs, wings—but his front wings showed flecks of white plus a small blocked pattern of apricot-yellow, and his hind wings were splashed with silver-white on the underside.

I searched my field guide and read of the skippers: ". . . positive identification of every specimen is a practical impossibility." Not promising. I leafed through the plates expecting nothing, but found a more-than-reasonable facsimile of my battling butterfly. That silvery splash on his hind wings is the identifying mark. He is a silver-spotted skipper. "Decidedly pugnacious," says the entry, further nailing him down.

At that very moment he sent two more butterflies (American coppers) on their way. They had been flitting just above the lawn grasses fully fifteen feet from his flowery pedestal, but he could not tolerate even their tiny intrusion.

I closed the guide and the skipper took off after a white cabbage butterfly fluttering between sunshine and shadow fully twenty-five feet away. He chased her into the shadows of the woods and returned to his tower.

I watched him, then, chasing flying insects of every size and description, and it seemed that the closer they approached his citadel the farther he chased them, and the farther away they were the shorter was his pursuit. I began to discern a pattern in his sallies and to realize that he was defending a territory with a definite size and a certain shape. The wall of the house formed one long straight boundary behind him while the other boundary, much in need of guarding, was a curved line with a radius extending into the lawn about thirty feet from the top of the hosta spike.

A red-spotted purple drifted in to drink at the dribble of water from the hose against the wall and the skipper dropped swiftly upon its back and sent it flying off.

Next came a bumblebee. The skipper watched her come until she was scarcely five feet from the hosta blossoms, then he flew at her, striking her in the face and pouncing upon her back. Perhaps because she was so close to her goal, or perhaps because she was a bumblebee, she refused to be driven away. She ignored the assaults, flew straight ahead, and entered the first open flower she came to, alighting upon its extended white stamens and disappearing into its lavender cone.

The skipper flew back to his post and watched with studied nonchalance the bumblebee's officious going-into and bumbling backing-out-of every open blossom on the ten tall spikes.

Some thirty minutes and almost as many pursued insects later, a large carpenter bee, closely resembling the bumblebee, also visited the hosta blossoms. She cut into the nectar tube of each open flower while the skipper scrutinized every move but made no attempt to stop her.

It was scarcely that the skipper feared the sting of the bumblebee, for he consistently chased honey bees, paper wasps, mud wasps, white-faced hornets and yellow jackets out of his territory, although only the honey bee had any interest in his blossoms.

And he *was* guarding a food source. Every thirty minutes or so he would perch on the tips of the stamens in one flower or another, unroll his proboscis, and sip from the ever-refilling nectar cups. What a nourishing drink that nectar must be, I thought, to sustain such a series of thrusts and sallies, such long-continued sentry duty, so many reconnaissance flights.

He had been on guard for five hours when a female ruby-throated hummingbird darted in and began feeding among the hostas. The skipper obviously saw her for he kept adjusting his position to face her, exactly, however she moved. But he did not attack her—not until she approached the plant upon which he sat. Then he launched himself directly at her face. The hummingbird, to my surprise, backed off, and flew away across the lawn with the pugnacious skipper close behind.

Ready, now, for some lunch, I laid down my gardening tools and started toward the house. Suddenly, without warning, that brown butterfly hit me atop the head with all the force of his infinitesimal weight and kept hitting me repeatedly. I could feel him smacking my hair and hear the papery clatter of his wings as he drove me to the door.

That afternoon, in addition to chasing insects, he turned on Kela, attacking her every time she walked by the hostas. He hit her in the middle of the back, stamping angrily on her long white hair and staying well away from her lazily snapping jaws.

He darted toward the two cats every time they came in sight, too, but he cut short his thrusts well out of reach of their swiftly striking claws.

A decidedly pugnacious butterfly, but one whose pugnacity is well-salted with regard for the well-being of a certain silver-spotted skipper.

Sounds of a Misty Morning

When Kela and I left the house one warm and quiet August morning, our world was narrowed to close walls of mist and the ribbon of earth we walked upon. In the cottony stillness we ran down the gravelled lane, paused beside the mailbox to listen for an unlikely car, then crossed the blacktop road and trotted down the hill through the cornfield. Down between two curving rows of tassel-topped green that reached high above my head and brushed us both with dripping, saw-edged leaves. Green corn, brown earth, white dog, gray mist. And nothing else.

We turned west at the pasture fence, following its dark, familiar line, and Kela inspected the tracks of pheasants, raccoons, foxes and dogs in the soft earth. Wherever I could see over, under, around or through the fenceline hedge of blackberries, mulberries and multiflora roses, I peered intently into the pasture trying to locate the dog-hating cattle; but all I could see was thickening mist.

At our special entrance into this pasture Kela paused, head down, indicating to her well-trained mistress that the loose wire should be lifted that she might pass under. I hesitated. I could not see to the creek. As a matter of fact, I could scarcely see the great oak snag on the edge of the bramble swamp just off to my left, so how could I see a cow? For that matter, how could they see us?

Under the fence we went, across the marsh, through the reeds and the tear thumb and the laughing-faced monkey flowers; a brief play in the creek where it gurgled over stones among the trees, and under the great down log; then into the marsh on the other side where the blue vervain blossomed higher than my head and where three green frogs twanged their loose vocal cords, one note at a time. One sang bass, one baritone, one tenor, and they never sang together, but always in one, two, three order, and each one a single note apiece. They made, I realized, the only sounds we'd heard since leaving the house.

We passed beyond the froggy voices, threading the narrow cow-path between the wide reaches of the hill-pasture on our right and the dark silences of the fog-swirled swamp on our left, walking enclosed in a cube of gray space.

Out of the eerie emptiness and silence of the swamp one cardinal suddenly whistled—just one full and startling call, then deeper silence fell behind it. Now and then the great bulk of a swamp oak loomed out of the mist like a giant shadow and faded behind us, or the trailing outline of a willow, obscure and indistinct. Old logs rotting into the soil, black with wetness. Dark stumps, broken trees, trailing vines of honeysuckle and creeper. Smell of swampwater; of decomposing leaves; of thick greenness. I spoke to Kela twice—but I whispered.

Now the Y-shaped snag of an old maple tree loomed out of the fog, and as we paused beneath it we saw a mother raccoon with three puppy-sized youngsters playing about in its double top. The mother, when she saw us, climbed, unhurried, to the broken crest. There, black hands down across her chest, she watched us, wary, not panicked, but concerned for her babies. She chirred so softly my ears scarcely caught the sound, but the two little ones directly below her clambered upward immediately, spraddle-legged, tails dragging, to sit like kittens on the splintered edges of the break. The mother's deft hands half-lifted, half-shoved first one babe and then the other into the dark opening below her, and the two were gone from my sight.

She chirred again, and once more my ears barely caught the murmur of it; and the little one opposite her, on the other arm of the Y, clambered down into the cleft and scrambled the length of him up toward her, twenty feet above. But his mother, without ruffling a hair, chirred again, and he slid back to the divide and disappeared into a hidden opening I didn't know was there.

Now, with her little ones safely stashed in the maple's

vault, the mother raccoon sat at apparent ease, braced between the broken top and the only leafed-out branch on the tree, and with bright, dark, interested eyes, watched us walk away.

We climbed beyond the swamp, following the course of a mossy runlet, listening to its murmurs, its whispers, its gurgles and its tinklings.

Up the round of the curving hill and into the sassafras lines at its top, winding on the cowpath there. An abrupt turn to the right from the path and we dropped into the cut between woods and peak. I could see nothing in any direction except down—to Kela and the short-cropped grass beneath our feet. We made the short, steep climb to the peak, and there stood a thistle plant, grand and lonely and shrouded in mist. I strained my eyes trying to see the cattle, the thirty or forty red-gold Guernseys I knew were abroad somewhere in this wide-flung pastureland. I saw nothing but whiteness and the foggy thistle.

Kela led off, slightly to our left, half-running down the long graceful sweeps of the east-lying hill. We could hear nothing but our own footsteps, see nothing but a fog-draped milkweed or another thistle, smell only the wetness of the white walls through which we passed and the grassy, milky, cow-y smell of the pasture. All in silence. All in whiteness. And only because I know this neighbor's dearly-loved land with a deep, inwoven knowing, did I know where we walked and in what direction we were turning.

We reached the bottom of the hill, crept beneath a fence, crossed the marsh, and romped again in the ripply creek. We leaped its washed clay banks, rustled through the dripping corn, and, wet to the skin, walked back to the house, wrapped in August morning mist every footstep of the way.

Spiders by the Thousands

According to authorities who look into such matters there are some twenty thousand spiders on every acre of open land. I am convinced that the count is correct to the very last spider and that, in September, all twenty thousand of them are members of the Argiope tribe, in gypsy-type encampment.

They hang their webs by the thousands in the fallow fields, the marshes, the borders of the ponds. They hang them in every conceivable spot and at every possible angle, and when Kela and I walk out, no matter how carefully we thread our way, we rip these webs apart by the dozens, by the hundreds.

Most September mornings are wet with dew, and each single strand of the myriad spider webs is strung with crystal that sparkles in the sunlight and turns these wild pastures into a glistening Eden.

As we walk through the wet spider fields, the Argiopes (Argiope is the scientific name for the heavy-bodied, black-and-yellow garden spider and its more slender, lighter-hued cousin, the banded Argiope) leave off their breakfasting—or their waiting, or their sleeping—and plummet from their webs to the ground in a series of small plops! like a barrage of pebbles dropping steadily ahead of us.

But on mornings without dew, when the dry webs billow lightly about us, these same spiders sit calmly on their home cushions, napping or eating grasshoppers or moths, and give no indication that they are aware of our going by.

Long Septembers ago this puzzled me. It seemed strange that every spider in every field should fear us greatly one day and be without concern the next.

But one morning I paused before a giant web whose spirals, strung between a goldenrod and a boneset, must have been two feet across. Its owner had dropped to earth before we arrived and the unoccupied web shimmered in the pale light with countless drops of silver dew. I raised my hand, inadvertently breaking a single guy line to the web, and the whole lovely construction collapsed upon itself instantly—into a wet, sticky, gray-white blob that, fortunately, did not have a black-and-golden spider trapped within it.

Then I understood the series of plopping spiders on a dewy day. If I break a supporting line on a day without dew, the web sags a little, hangs askew, and even if half the web is ripped away the spider is safe enough on what remains. But, when every line of a web is heavy with dew, one snapped support throws it fatally out of balance and each overloaded line adds to the swiftness of the collapse.

Thus it was the security of her location that first commanded my interest in one particular black-and-yellow Argiope. She had hung her web between two sturdy asters at the corner of the pond, facing the open water, but protected from prevalent winds by the rise of the earthdam. She was set a little apart from the great congathering of her kin by a bramble tangle directly behind her that also made it unlikely her web would be destroyed by the blundering about of either earth or water creatures.

In addition, she was uncommonly large, especially for July when most Argiopes are not yet fully grown. Her body was one and one-quarter inches long, rounded and broad, and she measured four inches, exactly, from back feet to front ones. She was an Amazon of the Amazons, and with great originality I named her Argiope.

Sometime during the first week of August I noticed the tiny male and the primitive little web he had built against a lower corner of hers. At about the same time Argiope's body began to grow unbelievably larger. She became so distended, her skin so taut and shining, I thought she would explode.

On the morning of August 11, I found Argiope in her usual place, head downward in the zigzagged center of her wheel, her body shrunken and wrinkled. It took some minutes of uncomfortable searching before I found her egg-case hanging in the dark shelter of the brambles.

Within the next week the little male disappeared. Did she

eat him? I don't know. The male is devoured under laboratory conditions much more often than in the wild where there is plenty of room to escape. But, eaten or not, it makes little difference, for the male dies shortly after mating.

Whatever may have happened to him, the male disappeared, and I supposed Argiope's egg-laying was finished—one egg-case per spider is a general rule—but, surprisingly, she began to grow again. Not very much, though, and she had not nearly attained her former size when, on the morning of August 24, I found her shrunken again and a second egg case, every bit as large as the first, hanging near it under the bramble leaves.

Both egg-cases were a pale tan in color with shadings into a deeper brown. They were handsomely shaped, like narrow-necked jugs with round bottoms, and each one measured five-eighths of an inch in diameter and one and one-quarter inches from the tip of the neck to the bottom of the jug. Each little jug was held upright and in place by a remarkable number of filmy guy lines.

Only a few days after the second egg-case appeared, Argiope began to grow once more, but slowly this time, so that it is only now that she seems, again, in imminent danger of splitting.

One day soon she will present the world with her third egg-case and that, I should think, will be her last. She could, possibly, have time for one more egg-laying, but her remaining days are few. Whether frost comes early or late, she will begin, now, to grow weaker and more careless. She will eat less food and eat it less often. Her web will be torn or fall completely apart and she will not bother to build a new one. All around her all her tribe will be failing, too, and every glistening, spiralled web will become only dusty, twisted strings.

And one frosty morning Kela and I shall walk out and all the Argiopes will be gone from the gardens, the fallow fields, the marshes, and the borders of the ponds. But next summer's gypsy-camp assembly lies quietly waiting in thousands upon thousands of shiny egg masses securely stored away in thousands upon thousands of little brown jugs.

Drama on a Wooden Fence

he fence should have been painted early in the spring but other tasks and other interests had pushed the job aside. Summer had been a succession of rainy or steamy days, and it was not until a glorious October afternoon that I began to paint the scarred old pickets.

Being a perfectionist only in certain well-defined directions, I painted the fence, to my own satisfaction at least, while letting the October day keep my five senses busy and my gypsying mind wandering on a hundred vagrant trails.

Even the odor of paint could not prevent the nutty smells of the close-by woods or the fruity smells of the apple trees or the ripe Autumn smells of the weeds and grasses from reaching my nostrils.

Bob Whites whistled their anxious covey-calls from the orchards and the hills. Blue jays screamed and scolded and pounded sunflower seeds into the crevices of white oak bark. Gray squirrels chattered and quacked and bounced frost-ripened hickory nuts down the dark limbs to the ground.

The dogwoods were purple-leaved and scarlet-berried along the edges of the woods. Shadows shifted and flowed on the grass when cool-tipped breezes lifted their leaves. A thousand milkweed silks drifted on the light-drenched air.

And then a gravid, green-bronze mantis nearly four inches long landed on the unpainted plank at the top of the fence and brought my attention closer to my job.

She wandered restlessly back and forth along the top of the fence for several minutes. Suddenly she became aware of me. She stalked to the edge of the fence and peered down at my kneeling form. She cocked her green-button head first to one side and then to the other and stared at me with an intensity that made me acutely self-conscious. Could she see the whole of me? I wondered. If not, how much could she see with those great compound eyes? Was she studying me? Was she mystified by this un-typical, non-food-gathering, non-shelter-building activity of mine? Was she trying to classify me?

I try not to be anthropomorphic, especially when considering a consciousness so foreign as that of an insect, but this mantis was something else. For two full hours she followed me along the fence, never more than two feet behind me, usually close at my side, not taking her eyes from me the entire time. She scrutinized every move I made, stared at my face and my paint-spattered coveralls, and seemed to interest herself in what I was doing, which included scrupulously not painting the top of the fence.

For two hours neither she nor I had looked at another creature, but now I saw, a few feet ahead of us, a small dark spider begin to build its frail web in the angle between the top-most plank and a fencepost. It spun swiftly and in less than twenty minutes it had suspended three fine lines and hung a sticky trap within them.

Building completed, it had scarcely retired to an upper corner when a housefly blundered into the snare. The spider dashed to the spot, tied down the struggling captive with a few well-placed strands of silk, and began to dine, first clipping off the pale wings and allowing them to spiral to the ground.

When the spider had finished its meal it sat back and wiped its face with its front legs.

Now, up behind the complacent spider crept the praying mantis. She stalked upon her four angular legs with sinister intent. Her head was up, her eyes were fixed upon the spider. She held her short, saw-toothed front legs folded below her face in a worshipful attitude. She was ready for the kill.

With a graceful motion so swift I'm not sure I saw it, the mantis reached forward and grasped the spider in her spiny arms. I know I witnessed no *coup de grâce*, but perhaps the knife-sharp grip stunned the little spider. At any rate, the mantis proceeded at once to eat it, from the edges in, as though it were a slice of watermelon.

When she had completed her meal, the mantis, in turn, washed her saw-tooth weapons and her face. Cat-like, she cleaned her front feet with her mouth, then rubbed them over her face and over her eyes again and again. When she had bathed, she took one more look at me, then spread her green-bronze wings and flew heavily off, dropping into the yellow chrysanthemums below the fence.

I confess that I watched these episodes in complete fascination with no thought to rescue either fly or spider. I considered that to really complete the drama a pigeon should fly down and eat the mantis; I, in turn, should eat the pigeon; then some larger animal should leap the fence and swallow me. Nothing of the sort occurred, however, and the food chain, for the time being, ended there.

But two questions press at the back of my mind: First, why did the mantis stay with me all that long afternoon? and, second, did the mantis feel that she had eaten only a spider, or did she realize she had also eaten a fly?

Swashbuckling Crows

The first time I heard a raven calling, the bird was sitting high on the sun-drenched rimrock of the Utah-Arizona border holding a fascinated conversation with his own echo.

The last time I heard a raven calling, the bird sat high in the top of a leafless maple amid my neighbor's hillside corn stubble, apparently enjoying the resonant qualities of his solo voice under the low gray skies of a cold and somber November afternoon.

I heard him calling when we left the house, and although I had never known a raven in this vicinity, I recognized his voice and set out to locate him. It took a few false starts in several directions, some unnecessary wading about in the marshes, and a few visits, by Kela, to neighborhood groundhog holes, before I discovered where the bird was perched.

All in all, some twenty or thirty minutes elapsed before we began the gradual climb to where the hidden bird continuously repeated his loud and rusty "Cr-r-ruck!"

The bird was big and black, and we had just reached a spot where my eyes could begin to question whether his tail was squared off or wedge-shaped when he took off with flapping wings and a loud, triumphant "Caw!" that rang in my disappointed ears like the derisive laughter it probably was.

Over on the stony knoll a barred owl chose that moment to slip from the green boughs of one pine tree to the heavier cover of another, and the crow launched himself in that direction with a series of wild caws that was like the skirling of pipes in the highlands.

Up from the woods and the swamps and the hidden coves of the mile-long valley his black-kilted clansmen rallied to his call. With flapping wings and strident voices they converged upon that pine and upon that brown-eyed owl, but not as blood-roused highlanders, to do battle. These came to jeer and to cat-call, to strut and to swagger, to mock and to swashbuckle—but not to fight.

In a hopeless attempt to get away from the noise the owl moved to another limb, to another tree, and even, eventually, to another woods, but every time he stirred, the encircling mob whipped itself into a new frenzy of ringing insult, and protest, and anti-owl opinion.

After an hour or more of clangorous excitement, the crows began to tire of the game and to go off, one by one, to their private pursuits, and the owl flew, unmolested, back to the pines to take up his interrupted nap where he had left it. With the probable exception of the barred owl's sensibilities and the sensitive ears of a few of his neighbors, no one had been hurt and the crows had had a great afternoon of blustering fun.

On still another November day when high gray clouds streamed across the sky in a steady, almost violent wind from the west, I saw six crows above our woods battling upward against that wind, climbing it, being tossed over on their sides, being pushed back twenty feet at a time, but still climbing. They climbed until they were above the horizon hills, and there, as at a signal, they all let go, let themselves be whirled about, went slipping, sliding, sailing down the long wild hill of the wind—back across the dark woods, the frozen marshes, the dun-colored fields—and dropped precariously to shelter among a grove of pin oaks more than a mile away.

Six times that afternoon I saw those same six crows repeat the strenuous climb for no reason at all except a wild, exciting slide down an invisible, mile-long hill.

But crows are always having fun. They are crafty, blatant, ebullient clowns enjoying themselves, whether they are building a nest, chasing a fox, stealing an egg, cawing from a treetop, or flying reconnaissance across the countryside.

And it is precisely this outright, loudmouthed quality of having a ball, plus their apparent intelligence, plus their casual, shoulder-shrugging disregard for man, that brings fiery revenge and thundering warfare upon their little feathered heads.

Hawks and owls and eagles may be hunted and killed by certain angry people, but not usually with such personal animosity, such single-minded determination to exterminate as is accorded to crows. But then, hawks and owls and eagles go about the business of securing a living in a respectably serious manner. They take their chances as they come, and not one of them ever laughed in the face of a man.

If crows would only, quietly, pull up and eat the soft, sweet germinating corn in the nation's fields, if they would, then, fly off in terror at the sight of an approaching human, if they would show some hesitation, some respect for the ingenious scarecrows erected to frighten them. But crows parade along the greening rows, preen their black feathers in the morning sun, flaunt their pirating presence in every way they know how. They post sentries in trees and on fenceposts and, when warned, flap slowly away—just beyond range of whatever weapon the pursuing human defender happens to be carrying.

And the scarecrow that can actually scare a crow has not yet been invented.

There is so much we do not know about crows. We do not know for certain whether they mate for life or for a season. We think both males and females concern themselves with nesting duties, but we aren't sure about it. We know that a crow's caws carry a multitude of messages to other crows, the meaning dependent upon the inflection, the tone, the speed, and the series in which the caws are uttered. We know they can make a great many other harsh, grating and throaty sounds. We know they can learn to repeat human words, without their tongues being slit, for all crow talk comes from the bottom of the windpipe. But we do not know whether or not crows sing musical songs to one another when they are alone.

There are ornithologists who hoot at the very idea of musical tones from those rasping throats, and others who insist they have heard sweet singing when they were well-hidden from a pair, or a flock, of crows. For myself, I have never managed to get within earshot of a crow without his knowing I was there; but I am willing to believe that big, tough, talented, swashbuckling crows can sing sweetly enough, if they want to.

When Clocks Go Wrong

$\mathcal{D}$ay by day, through all the months since the longest day of the summer solstice, the sun has been journeying southward and the hours of daylight have steadily diminished by sixty seconds in every twenty-four hours.

Sixty seconds. A mere breath of light they seem, imperceptible to most of us until thirty days, or sixty days, or even until ninety days have passed. Then suddenly daylight is clipped off at the end a little sooner than we expected, and abruptly we are made aware that a change of season is upon us.

But other living things have known, deep within their organisms, that fewer moments of light and lesser amounts of heat have been falling upon the earth, and each one has responded to these changes after his own kind. Fruits have ripened; flowers have blossomed and set their seeds; a majority of insects have laid their eggs and their worn-out bodies have fallen to earth.

Migrating birds have followed the sun southward, and thousands of animals have eaten and grown fat for the long weeks of hibernation, or have stored food in hopefully accessible places against those same long weeks of cold and storm.

"Biological clocks" we call the systems of inner prompting that make the groundhog over-eat, the gray squirrels bury nuts in the earth, and maple leaves develop abscission layers as the light begins to fail—and then direct seeds to sprout, eggs to hatch, and frogs to mate as light and heat return at the opposite side of the year.

Fifty degrees Fahrenheit seems to be the critical line, the magic demarcation on the temperature scale. Although creatures great and small have been making their preparations for the winter for weeks or months before, these processes seem suddenly to accelerate, or, in many cases, to reach their final stage when temperatures drop, and stay, below that critical point. And, in the spring, awakening life fairly burgeons into the open air when the temperatures rise and stay above that same magic degree.

It is true that December is, most often, a winter month of cold and darkness and storm, when hibernating wildlings sleep the deep sleep of winter torpor, and non-hibernating creatures move warily, hampered by the weather, amid their hungry predators.

But sometimes a wintry December brings, also, a day or even a week of surprising gentleness, of sunshine and blue skies, of temperatures that rise above fifty degrees Fahrenheit—especially on dark tree trunks and in sheltered places that face the southward sun. And because of that magical measure of heat some biological clocks go off too soon; some little creatures are triggered into activity when they should be lying low, and lives are lost as nature weeds out another lot of living things with poor survival habits.

For some animals the warmth is merely a welcome reprieve from the winter's cold and they hunt or flee in greater comfort, but they break no laws. Their clocks have not gone wrong.

On warm and gentle December days chipmunks come up from their dark bedrooms and race about in the dry leaves on the woods floor, and gray squirrels dash playfully along lofty highways. Cottontails and white-tailed deer skitter and prance on their own hidden pathways in the hours of dawn and of twilight; and opossums, raccoons, foxes and skunks prowl comfortably through the night.

There are others, though, enjoying the warmth and freedom, whose stories end quite differently.

For three days now the red line on the thermometer outside my window has touched the bar marked fifty, and has sometimes pushed several degrees beyond that mark before the close of day.

Today, as I walked through the woods, I saw a blue-edged mourning cloak butterfly drifting down a sunlit corridor as though spring were here. It is using energy, consuming its little store of fuel, and there is not a sap-bleeding tree in all this

December woods, not a drop of food to re-fill that dark butterfly body.

Out on the hilltop, beyond the woods, a bright yellow common sulphur butterfly danced across the old hayfield looking as cheerfully at home as though the sun-sparkled brown world were filled with clover blossoms. Common sulphurs usually hibernate as pupae, protected from winter weather by the hard shell of the chrysalis; and only sometimes, and only perhaps, hibernate successfully as adults. This one, with a biological clock so faulty that it split its shell and emerged from its chrysalis in December, is obviously going to have to hibernate as an adult or, most likely, to die in the attempt. There is no food, now, for a little body that feeds upon the nectars of the clover family.

Late this afternoon a hop merchant butterfly fluttered with a papery rustle of his bright-orange, many-angled wings against the opened casement windows of my study. Hop merchants, like mourning cloaks, normally winter as adults; but those whose clocks allow them to go flitting about the countryside on sunny winter days are likely to find themselves out of fuel and far from proper shelter when the warm recess is over.

Over-wintering female wasps, and houseflies, and ladybugs come creeping out of the cracks and crannies where they have successfully sheltered thus far, and fly about or sun themselves on the south side of the house; and I will find their frozen bodies lying on the stones in little windrows when the weather changes back to winter.

Lilacs and forsythia often put forth a few blossoms if the weather stays warm enough for long enough. We almost expect it of them. But in the orchard this afternoon I found two pink and white blossoms on the red astrakhan apple tree. They were as fresh and as fragrant as any blooms of May-time, and a honeybee from a nearby hive rolled among their stamens.

The honeybee probably got back to its hive with the pollen it collected, but the apple blossoms are doomed. They can never develop a fruit, never set a seed. Nature has no more use for a Maryland apple orchard that blossoms in December than she has for a hornet that attempts a paper cone out of season.

Winter Buds

The light of the low-hanging January sun, beaming through the furry buds of the peach trees and the nectarines, turning them to pussy-willow silver, signals a reminder that the vegetable world is only lying low.

Within these slender, pointed bits of fuzz now twinkling in the winter breeze, all the twigs and leaves and blossoms of the summer orchard are neatly folded, coiled and fitted. They wait there, sustained by infinitesimal amounts of air and moisture enfolded with them in the protection of their furry coats. I suspect that if they could be told, they would completely disbelieve the prodigious activity to which they will be awakened a dozen weeks from now.

All tree buds are protected by furry coats or by scales of one kind or another to bring them through the ice and snow and bitter winds of winter. Dry, cold winds are a greater hazard to winter buds than frost and snows can ever be. Their outer coverings shed the dampness of rains and snows but cannot prevent dehydration from prolonged dry winds, especially in periods of excessive cold when the earth is deep-frozen so that the roots cannot replenish the helpless buds.

Birds—grouse, and quail, and pheasants—feast on winter buds, especially aromatic kinds like sassafras, birch and poplar. Squirrels and rabbits eat them, too, but none is likely to eat so many from one tree that they cause serious damage, unless, of course, it is a seedling tree, shrub or vine. For all woody plants preserve their livingness in the compact enclosures of all their winter buds.

You can see how compact these enclosures are if you remove one of the twin buds from the twig tip of a lilac bush, open it, and, with a magnifying glass, look at its contents. The infinitesimal beginnings of the profusion of flowers that make up one bunch of lilacs are enclosed in a single diminutive winter bud. And so it is with other panicled blooms, with grapes and locusts and buckeyes, whose leaves and flowers and twigs and stems are all folded down together, packed away in diminutive containers, ready to rise with the rising sap.

At the tip of a twig on the tulip tree is an egg-shaped bud covered by two glossy, red-and-lavender scales clamped together like the beak of a long-billed bird. Packed inside is envelope after envelope of tiny folded leaves, and its opening in spring is like the car in the circus from which an impossible number of clowns escapes.

The brown winter bud on the persimmon tree has only two scales, too, but they are simply overlapped, not clamped together. There are olive buds in the hedge row nestling in resin, glistening black; and hazel buds dressed in russet and green like Robin Hood's merry men.

The flat flower buds on the dogwood tree look like praying mantis heads in spite of the difference in coloring. The four gray covers hold the tiny cluster of true flowers safe from winter storms, but when spring arrives they vary the usual procedure for bud scales and, instead of drying up and falling off or being pushed aside, they grow. Their veins open to the sap and they soften, and spread, and stretch, and turn white, and become the four attention-getting "petals" of the dogwood flowers. The gray color is still there, staining the tips of the broad white bracts.

The leaf buds of the dogwood tree have their two scales clamped together like the buds of the tulip tree. But when these red-brown buds with their pea-green bases burst open, they reveal only the pointed tips of two green leaves which to some people look like forked tongues, but to me are minute green candle flames lighting up the springtime woods.

Oak buds and hickory buds are numerous in this climax forest on whose edge I live, the buds varying for white oak and pin oak, for shagbark and pignut; and if I could only remember the variations I could always and easily separate the species. Of course white oak and shagbark hickory are also identifiable by their ever-present bark. The white oak and the red oak families can be separated by their leaves. There are differences in the acorns from one oak species to another just as there are differences in the nuts of the various hickory species. Identification by bud is the hard way—and sometimes I tell myself that I don't go around trying to recognize people by their fingerprints, and, after all, I do know an oak tree from a hickory tree. But these signature buds are fascinating.

The terminal buds on hickory twigs (except for one or two species) are stout and round and tapered to their tips. They are downy and light-colored—like buffy, silky suede—and are easily the most noticeable buds in all the winter woods.

Oak buds, on the other hand, are small and reddish-brown, many-scaled and mostly hairy, and they are clustered on the twig tips. Within them are folded the two million or so leaves which clothe the oak in summer and the little gnarled twigs which grow into the supple gnarled branches which become the heavy gnarled limbs that mark the strong gnarled oak trees wherever we may see them.

The trees that grow on the banks of the streams in the marshes where I wander, the willows and the sycamores, distinct in so many ways from the forest trees, are distinctive, also, in the coverings of their winter buds. Only a single scale protects their enfolded greenery. A single scale, plastic, formed without a seam, is fitted over each miniature twig, each lilliputian, single-growing leaf.

The thin, pointed buds of the willow tree lie so close to the twigs from which they grow that they are almost invisible except that they are shiny and waxy and they gleam in the light of the winter sun.

But the buds of the sycamore, although they are only faintly glossy and their pale color is not conspicuous, stand out clearly on their twigs because of their jutting, conical shape. They look as though a fine nylon hood had been stretched and fitted about the underlying form. And when, in spring, the new twigs and leaves push forth, they rip their hoods right off at the bases and wear them askew until the dry and useless coverings are carried off by wind or rain.

Winter buds, with the scars of last year's leaves below them, are the individual signatures for every species of vine and shrub and tree. You will need a hand lens to read most of them, a good field guide to match them to, and a rejoicing in wintry winds to get you out among them; but your reward is a deeper understanding and a closer touch to the oneness of being alive.

The Second Secret of Skunk Cabbage

O ut in the marshes and the swamps, close against the edges of exposed gray rocks, in shallow depressions at the bases of knolls, on and between the unsteady hummocks that dot the wetlands, the pointed tips of skunk cabbage spathes are pushing up through the black frozen earth, through panes upon panes of glassy ice, through wet or powdery inches of snow, and out into the inhospitable air of gray and lowering February.

Like clusters of round-shouldered teepees they stand. Gray-green, yellow-green, splashed and mottled with purples and reds, burgeoning with life that cannot wait for the returning sun but must thaw the unready earth with its own self-generated radiance.

For within each of those teepees burns a fire, a feverish churning of growth and development, and its growing tip is twenty to twenty-seven degrees warmer than the winter air about it. Thus it melts the ice and the snow and the hard, frozen marshland. On a winter day when the thermometer registers twenty degrees Fahrenheit, the new-growing skunk cabbage out in the bottomlands is basking in its own nearly fifty degrees of warmth, manufacturing its own private springtime in the very midst of winter. And that is the first, well-documented secret that skunk cabbage holds to its pungent heart.

All processes of growth, whether in plant or in animal, generate heat; but the growing points of skunk cabbage seem to liberate greater amounts than other vegetation that has been checked. Whether the excess radiance is a matter of skunk cabbage metabolism or of the extra effort expended to push through the high resistance of frozen earth, I do not pretend to know.

Nor do I know why skunk cabbage begins to stir so early in the year. Presumably it is responding to the stimulus of the northerly swinging sun, but why does it rouse to so slight a sunning? From its earliest winter beginnings—hidden under the close-drawn draperies of its purpled cowl—to the wide-flung spreading of its huge, wavy-edged leaves in the heat of summer, it looks a tropical growth, one more to be expected in a fetid, leech-hung jungle than in the frozen expanses of a February marsh.

As a matter of fact, botanists say that the closest relatives of skunk cabbage do live in the steaming jungles of Malaya. They say, also, that skunk cabbage must have migrated north-ward through Asia, reached America by way of that much-traveled land bridge without which one wonders just how naked and alone the western hemisphere might have been, and, pushed southward by the glaciers, developed on the seaboards into two separate types which never, at any point, come within a thou-sand miles of meeting.

If skunk cabbage did do all that traveling from south-eastern Asia to northwestern America, it certainly didn't do it by itself and must have been carried by man on his own harried migrations. For food? Even Euell Gibbons, that indefatigable gatherer and eater of the edible wild, found it a most unpalatable dish. But Gibbons was a western man and the Oriental taste is for hotter foods than ours, so it may have come as a food item with the travelers. More probably, it traveled as a medicinal herb, for the American Indian is supposed to have used it widely both as a stimulant and as a narcotic.

Skunk cabbage belongs, of course, to the Arum family, which makes it a cousin to Jack-in-the-pulpit. The relationship is plain to see, when, wearing waterproof clothing, I kneel in the February marshes and peer through the narrow slit doorway of a four-inch leathery teepee. There, in the center of that shadowed interior, if the light falls properly, I can see the lone, thick-stemmed spadix with the knobbed head that is the blossom-ing member of this strange-mannered plant. Sometimes, even this early, I find the knob already covered with off-lavender blooms, and, occasionally, the off-lavender blooms already are hidden completely by the hazy netting of its straw-colored stamens and pistils.

If the flower petals are spread or even just beginning to open, and if the day is sunny, or the temperature approaches fifty, there, unbelievably, are the tiny carrion flies all ready to perform their nuptial duties for the skunk cabbage blossoms and to assure their own posterity.

The skunk cabbage spadix usually holds fifteen perfect flowers, each producing one large, black-brown seed. These fifteen seeds are embedded in the spherical surface of the fleshy knob which lies on the ground, whole and unblemished, long after purpled spathe and great summer leaves have all disappeared.

And thereby hangs a tale.

By the middle of July the skunk cabbage areas are made all but impassable by the thick press of brambles and the multitude of marsh-growing vegetation, most of which grows higher than my head; so I take easier, clearer routes through fields and pastures in late summer, autumn and early winter.

On a day late in August, two years ago, Kela and I were caught between ranks of most inhospitable farm animals, and we found it expedient to push our way through a thickly grown, unpastured marsh. And here, at the foot of a rocky knoll, I found several dark, full-seeded skunk cabbage knobs lying on the ground.

Kneeling to examine them, for I did not want to disturb in any way their probable sinking into their native ooze, I was amazed to discover there, just pushing through the surface, newly growing tips of skunk cabbage spathes. These were not the tiny growths of first-year seedlings but fully developing spathes of perennial skunk cabbage plants.

I came home and searched my books, went to the library and searched theirs, and all I found about skunk cabbage growth was the tale of its mid-winter appearance with the aid of self-generated heat.

Perhaps there was something unusual about the base of that knoll, so I visited other marshes and other points in this same marsh and found, over and over, the tips of skunk cabbage spathes penetrating the surface of the ground. The next fall I checked the marshes, and this past September I checked them again, and there they were, the same as before, a significant number of inch-high, leathery green points pushing through, getting a real head start, stealing a long march on their fellows.

Inadvertently, then, pushed by my neighbor's cattle, I discovered that skunk cabbage has a second secret: it sometimes begins its growth long before mid-winter. I'm not the only one who knows, I'm sure, but, somehow, the information hasn't gotten into the books, or into the books I've found. And so I openly share the knowledge of skunk cabbage's second secret, its secret secret, with you.

(After this article appeared in the Baltimore Sunday *Sun*, a reader most kindly pointed out to me that Mrs. William Starr Dana, in her book, *How to Know the Wild Flowers*, quotes Thoreau's *Journal* under date of October 31st: ". . . and see the brave spears of skunk cabbage buds already advanced toward a new year.")

Frogs in the Window Well

March. Waters and winds and mists and birds and sleet and frogs and mud and ice and flattened reeds and sedges.

But spring grows stronger day by day. Resurgent life pushes and throbs and nudges through the depths of the marshes, and the resurrection call goes out to all the scattered worshippers in woodland, thicket, copse and hollow—even to the sleepers in my window well who cannot return to the marshy places unless I lift them out and set them on their way.

Nearly every autumn several toads of several sizes drop into the window wells among the flagstones at the kitchen door and refuse to stay removed, so these hibernators I expect and look out for when spring is warm and really here. I place a pie pan of water there, quite early, just in case I don't notice when the first ones come up from their earth dens under the leaves.

But, even though I had already installed the pan of water, I was surprised to hear a hop! hop! hop! in those dry leaves just a few days after the first peeper song.

I crept softly, on hands and knees, over the flagstones reaching the edge of the window well just in time to see a miniature, buffy frog slip under a curled oak leaf. I scooped it up in my hand and held it there much against its tiny, thrashing will.

It was exactly the color of the pale undersides of the oak leaves that had swirled, six or eight inches deep, into the window well during the winter, and it had a definite, though somewhat spread-eagled, brown X on its back. *Hyla crucifer*. Spring peeper. It was so tiny, so delicately put together, and so desperately struggling to escape I was afraid I would injure it just by holding it.

But hold it I did, and looked it over well, for it isn't often I can close my hands on such an exquisite minikin. Its snippet of a buff nose came to a rounded point under high-perched eyes brightly edged in gold. One brown polka-dot marked the space between each two lines of its cross, and narrow bands of brown decorated its frantically springing thighs. The soft skin of its underparts was finely granular, beigey-white with a hint of greenish, and its wrinkled throat was lightly touched with yellow. No webbing at all between its long fingers and only a trace between its toes. Fingers and toes so delicate, so fine, and the climbing discs upon them infinitesimal but distinct. The whole adult peeper so minute it hid itself completely under the end of my thumb.

The day was warm and drizzly and the time was five in the afternoon. Little frogs by the tens of thousands were singing from all the marshlands hereabouts, and I took my newly-risen peeper down to the pasture fence and set it free in a drift of winter leaves.

I came back to the window well, lifted the pan of water and spied another peeper beneath a floating leaf. This one was even tinier, scarcely half as long, and much more docile than the first. It sat upon my open hand and looked about, and made not the slightest attempt to escape. Like the first frog, this one had a sprawling X upon its back. But it had a brushmark of red on its underside, and its wrinkled throat—the thin skin of its vocal sac—was dark. A male spring peeper.

A pair of peepers! For one long moment I considered fitting up the old aquarium for the two of them. But the miniscule peeper, indifferent to fateful decisions, began to explore the darkness inside my jacket sleeve. His dainty feet lightly touched my arm at every hop, and he nestled comfortably into the crook of my elbow—and I took him down to the pasture fence and released him.

Almost a week later, in the middle of the morning, I discovered a third little frog hiding under the leaves which now nearly filled the water pan. He was the same size as the first peeper, but his dark brown skin color practically obliterated the darker lines upon his back.

He snuggled quietly in my hand and I held him there in its warmth, each of us in our own way enjoying a rare moment of quasi-rapport between amphibian and mammal. I decided to wait until the safer evening hours to release him into the marshes, and, as I opened my hand to put him back into the window well, I was amazed to see that his skin had lightened to the palest beige and that the scattered markings on his back formed, not an X, but three narrow stripes from neck to vent. Another brown stripe extended, unbroken, the length of each side from nose to groin, and a fine white line marked his upper lip.

This little frog was not a peeper at all. He was an Upland Chorus Frog, another early riser, whose vibrant, repeated "cr-r-r-reeks," rising in pitch on the "eeks," blend delightfully with the tinkling sleigh bells of the peepers, and give the jubilant choruses around the ponds and puddles a rising and falling variety.

As I reached to place my chorus frog back in the water pan, he leaped from my hand to the white-painted window sill and crept into a shadowed niche where he promptly turned a pale pinkish- or purplish-gray.

Late that afternoon when rain began to fall and the singing in the watery lowlands had reached a wild crescendo, I went to release my newest frog into his fitting social milieu. I lifted the wet oak leaves from the pan and beheld *two* little chorus frogs stretched out full length in the water.

This newest frog was a dainty, half-inch miniature of the other; this one too was dark, dark brown on the wet, brown leaves and palely beige on the palm of my hand where both sat comfortably, side by side, and gravely studied the drab March land with bright little gold-rimmed eyes.

Reluctantly, yearningly, I released the two of them into their wild, wet world and watched them leap away to take their proper froggy places in the beginning-of-the-world cantata rising now from all the congregations gathered in the marshes.

April's Quiet Carnival

pril is as colorful a month as October, but not everyone
is aware of it, for April paints with a delicate touch while October goes in for the most flamboyant of colors. April's pastels are
hidden away, have to be looked for, have to be sought, quite
often afoot; but October flaunts her banners along every lane
and every highway, and the most uninterested rider is fairly
dazzled by the brilliance.

April is extravagant. April takes miniature buds and miniscule leaves, ripples them over bare twigs and branches, lays a
rainbow haze on every wooded hilltop, then scarcely allows it to
stay for a week.

October is frugal. October spectacularly trims the trees,
uses only full-grown, full-painted leaves, and lets the show go
on for two weeks, three weeks, or four.

October uses gold and purple, and scarlet and brown, yellow and orange, and salmon and rust. The forests are bold and
cushioned and dense.

April's colors run to amber and coral and rose, to amethyst
and honey and lemon and sand. Misted shades, tree-shaped,
indefinite, they are nonetheless distinct. Whole woodlands
picked out in feather-stitched trees. But the eye must be quick
to see them, for given three days of sunlight and shower, the
soft-tinted leaves will stretch out their lobes and turn ten
thousand practical shades of green. Every distinctive celebrant
tree will disappear into a chlorophyl forest and take up its serious
season's work of forming substantial sugars and starches from
intangible mixtures of sunlight and water and air.

October's flowers throng the earth in great patches of
mostly purple and gold. April practices a prodigal subtlety. Blossoms are scattered with a lavish hand, but they are tinted in the
tenderest tones. They grow, most of them, close to the ground,

beneath the trees, behind the rocks, and only the open eye may see and only the seeker may find.

From Maine to the Mississippi, on woodland slopes under leafless trees, those hairy little primitives, the hepatica, are the first to bloom; scattered blossoms or clumps upon clumps of bloom in pink, purple, or lilac, or lavender, or white, or blue. I'm down in the mould among them, sniffing to find the fragrant ones, for, though fragrance comes in all the colors, not all the colors are always fragrant. The scent is worth searching for, even creeping on hands and knees. It smells of earth, dry leaves, and violets. It is enticing and elusive. I can never breathe it deeply enough because the fragrance is lost before the breath is fully drawn.

And there is rue anemone, frail and delicate, thin stemmed, top-heavy with its leaves and its three white (rarely pink) blossoms. Storms can flatten it upon the ground and it will rise, when the storm is gone, to dance in the breezes and swing on the winds, to waft its pollen among its neighbors lest visiting insects fail at the task. Wood anemone, just as frail, just as delicate, but solitary-flowered, usually blooms as rue's companion, and one is often mistaken for the other by unpracticed searchers.

Bloodroot daisy rises in the woods with its tender bud wrapped in the protective round of a sturdy leaf, but the bud pushes above the gray-green blanket and opens its squared-off flower there. One leaf, one flower. But the flowers are large, and they blossom in close-growing profusion so that whole sweeps of woodland glow with these breeze-ruffled daisies. But they remain so short a time. Their slender petals are weakened by heat, bruised by rain and beaten by wind, so that it is only in the gentlest of April weather that their blossoming is prolonged. Mostly they are white, sometimes pink or lilac, but their centers are always deepest gold.

Golden, too, are the tips of the dutchman's breeches that grow in patches among the stones on sunlit woodland hillsides. They have fern-cut leaves and dainty, white blossoms that dangle from gracefully curving stems. It seems to me that if they had to be named for clothing at all, they should have been classed with feminine frippery and not with masculine workaday

wear. These blossoms fade quickly in heat or in wind, and often
are gone in two days or three.

Pussytoes and bluets grow on open hillsides and in low,
grassy meadows, and are almost stepped on before they are seen.

The silver tufts of pussytoes open at the ground from the
center of silky, silver-leaved rosettes. They are long-lasting and
they keep growing taller. They are never flamboyant and they
soon lose their silver, but their summer selves are far more apparent than when they first open in April's spring show.

Countless frail bluets mass in small profusion on wet hillsides and in low fields and meadows. They catch the eye of a
passerby as only a nebulous milky-blue blur. Their four delicate
petals, which are actually lobes, may be white or lilac or a soft
tone of blue, but the tiny flower tube is always yellow. Each
demure little blossom sits atop a fine, clear stem only two or
three inches above the ground. In spite of heat, or wind, or
flooding, or the heavy footfalls of cattle or men, this fragile blue
carpet often blossoms into July.

And there are violets. How many species? Once I set out
to identify them all. The whites and the yellows were not too
difficult to name, but the blues had me baffled in very short
order. Some of them matched their descriptions superbly—birds-
foot violet, common blue, arrow-leaved violet, downy blue—
but others did not match a single portrait that any of the field
guides or the botanists devised. "Most violets," I learned,
"hybridize freely." Then I stopped trying to identify the violets.

But known, or unknown, white or yellow or one of the
blues, no April violet flaunts its colors to one who hurries on
his way.

The pale pink bells of spring beauty and toothwort, the
fragrant pink blooms of trailing arbutus, tall green spathes of
Jack-in-the-pulpit, red-brown wild ginger hiding under the
leaves, the blooms of half a hundred other species—all are pale,
or low, ephemeral, or hidden.

April is festive and lavish and lovely, but, unlike October,
April exacts a price of admission to her show. April demands a
measure of effort, a close participation on the part of anyone
who wishes to see.

When Gray Squirrels Go A-Wooing

When spring comes late and April leaves are only a flush of green on the woods trees, the courtships of the gray squirrels are open to my view in far greater detail than probably the squirrels could wish, yet they are always frustrating to me because, most of the time, I do not know which squirrel is which.

Is it the male who is chasing the female, or is the female driving the male to a standoff? Whoever is doing what, the two of them flow in long gray spirals up and down the hickory trunks and round and round on the brown woods floor. They chatter to one another as they skim along the slimmest of limbs, dash through the twiggiest of interlacing branches, and leap across chasms from tree to tree. Tails streaming, feet flying, directions are reversed; the chaser becomes the chased; and only a flicker of motion exchanges the roles. The whole courtship pursuit is a long, graceful maneuver, and its consummation is quiet and kind.

For April courtships are the second wooings of the year. The female has already reared one brood of little squirrels, and, it seems to me, she is neither so wild nor so lively as she was during the January chasings, after three or four months with no young in her nest.

Wintertime courtships are noisy and wild, with barkings and chatterings and a variety of quackings, with four or five squirrels participating in a single chase, and every chase flowing on and on for hours, and sometimes, it seems, for days.

I am never sure, in January, whether the chase is a territorial squabble, a game of tag, or a genuine courtship. Nor have I ever seen a mating in January or February, although the trees are bare, the squirrels just beyond my windows, and the chases constant. But baby squirrels arrive in neighborhood nests in February and March, so it is only that I am not patient enough, or not observant enough, or not, often enough, in the right place at the proper time.

But April wooings I have seen, from beginnings to consummations. I do not say "to endings" because I think that squirrel courtships do not always end with a single mating, although, I think, the partners remain the same through any particular seasonal courtship.

There is so much we do not know about gray squirrels—or any animal, for that matter. Gray squirrel ways, like human ways, are not completely covered by generalities. There are certain biological facts that, put to the test, can be proved over and over again. But the behavior of any individual squirrel, while it may follow the norm, may just as likely be an original variation on the theme.

For instance: The gestation period for gray squirrels is from forty to forty-five days. This is biological fact. All squirrel babies arrive in this world with bare pink skins, oversize heads, tiny bodies and stubby tails. Their eyes are sealed shut and their ears are closed and pressed tightly to their heads. This is fact.

Over and over again through every twenty-four hours the squirrel mother lies with her fluffy tail wrapped around her naked babies while they feed from the milk glands on her furry stomach. Every day she washes each baby from head to foot with her busy tongue while she strokes its growing body with her paws. This is the general pattern. Some mothers may be much more attentive than others to their babies.

For a courtship, the long, noisy and exciting chase is probably a standard, but I suspect that even the chase varies with the individuals doing the chasing. The gray squirrel pattern is surely used, but gray squirrel variations are personally endless.

Once, on an April morning, I leaned against the trunk of a sour gum tree near the creek in the woods and watched the curiosity of a Carolina wren bring it closer and closer to where I stood.

A dry clatter of leafless branches made me look up to the rim of the ravine to see a gray squirrel, who had just made a long leap from tree to tree, walk slowly in along a limb. She kept pausing to look back over her shoulder as though she were expecting something to follow her. She made two additional, lesser, leaps between trees and landed in the outer branches of a white oak, low on the side of the ravine just above where I stood.

As she paused there to look over her shoulder, we both heard the barking voice of an approaching squirrel. We heard the rattle of branches as he made his traverses, we saw him arrive at the top of the ravine, and we watched his graceful flying leaps and runnings until, very quickly, he stood among the white oak branches with her.

She ran to meet him. They touched noses. Briefly. Then she trotted off, not very fast, and he followed close behind. In this manner they traveled in silence up the trunk of the oak and out along a gnarled old limb. They mated near its end, among the juttings of its branches, then turned and walked slowly back the length of the limb. They climbed a few feet higher up the trunk and disappeared, together, through a knot hole, into the tree's interior.

On another April day, two lively gray squirrels chased each other round and round and up and down among the hickory, oak and tulip trees just inside the woods beyond my kitchen window. Thirty minutes of chattering chase among the trees, then a slowing at ground level, a touching of noses, and a tumbling mating among the brown leaves on the ground.

They rose, smoothed their ruffled coats, and, walking slowly together, his head against her shoulder or resting on her flanks, they came out of the woods onto the lawn. Here they paused, sat up on their haunches and, with arms hanging loosely on their chests, chattered amiably with one another, heads scarcely five inches apart.

Down again on all fours for probably fifteen feet, then up on their haunches for another brief and bright-eyed chatter.

When they started off this time he walked with surprising smoothness on only three feet. His right arm lay across her shoulders and they went on with their conversation as they walked to the woodpile and vanished among its dark and secret passageways.

The Rising of the Turtles

Box turtles are literally climbing out of the earth all around us on these warm May mornings; creeping out; blinking in the sunlight; their heavy-shelled bodies wavering forward and back on scaly legs scarcely used since last October.

Every domed brown-and-yellow carapace, or upper shell, is streaked with crumbly smears of earth, for every turtle has mined his way on a slanting, upward path from his winter den below the frostline. They started their climbs several weeks ago and have probably been lying close to the surface awaiting the just-right warmth and sunlight of today, or, more especially, the warm and gentle rain that fell last night.

For, just as on a certain, uncalendared afternoon in March ten thousand little frogs begin to sing in the marshes, so, on an unforetold morning in May, box turtles in lesser numbers begin to move about. They sometimes emerge when the temperature is only sixty degrees, but they do not move about very much until it reaches seventy, and they only become really active when the temperature is between eighty and eighty-five degrees. When it gets hotter than that they seek shelter from the heat and go back underground—estivate.

The temperature, now, is just above seventy, and the turtles move, one by one, into the dewy fields, leaving the marks of their slow progress behind them—smearings of mud, displacements of dew, a pressing-down of grasses. On a two-mile, meandering walk Kela and I found fifteen box turtles, the greatest number we have ever seen in a single morning.

Box turtles, no matter what their ages, eat earthworms and slugs, fruits and berries and mushrooms. They have horny jaw plates instead of teeth and they slice their food neatly into bite-size pieces and swallow it. Strawberries and fallen peaches are favorite foods. And so are mushrooms of all kinds. In fact, the flesh of box turtles is said to be poisonous to man because of the poisonous mushrooms they eat with impunity.

Kela pays little attention to them in these days of her adulthood. She ignores them, disdains them, does not trust them —these scaly creatures who hide away within their own bones —and it upsets her to see me pick them up.

But I persist in checking every box turtle I find. Not for its age. Those concentric circles on the shields of the shells are only fairly accurate up to the age of fifteen years, and, since box turtles are known to live for thirty or forty and up to a hundred years, why bother with a mere fifteen?

No, I am checking the secondary sex characteristics of each turtle. The edges of the male's carapace usually flare outward and sometimes curl upward while the female's flare only slightly, if at all. The male usually has red eyes and his head is brightly blotched or speckled with yellow while the female's head is usually plainer and her eyes are brown. These inconclusive variations would mean little except that the rear lobe of the male's plastron, or lower shell, is always concave while the female's is always flat or slightly convex.

The courtship of box turtles is a rough and noisy affair, with the female sequestered in her bony castle and the male seeking to storm it by force. He circles her, high on his legs, striking her shell with the flared edges of his own at every step. He clambers over her repeatedly from front to back, from side to side, the edges of his carapace bumping and rattling against hers and his plastron scraping over the ridges. He hammers the front of his shell against the sides of hers. He rakes her shell with his claws. The wild siege goes on for hours until the male is practically beside himself and his red eyes seem to gleam with demonic rage. It all ends with the drawbridge lowered and the besieging knight sitting vertically on the end of his shell behind his hard-won lady.

One warm evening Kela and I discovered a box turtle in the act of laying her eggs in a newly planted cornfield. She had dug a nest about three inches deep and three inches wide—just the length of her hind legs—in the loose soil; and slowly, slowly, while we watched, she dropped in three small, white, parchment-shelled eggs. That done, she stood staring fixedly at nothing, resting from her labors, her cloaca tensing and relaxing. I thought she might lay a few more eggs (box turtles lay as many as eight in a single clutch, and the usual number is four) but after a while her legs began to scratch the earth and she started the long process of filling in and smoothing over the nest. We didn't stay to watch. A box turtle spends at least one hour digging the nest and at least two hours covering and concealing it.

While the turtle brushed loose earth over her soft-shelled eggs, I marked the site with stones and an upright branch from a wildcherry tree. As I worked, Kela and I walked all about her but she was not disturbed. She appeared oblivious to her surroundings, in a mindless state bordering on hypnosis. She moved like an automaton, without meaning, without awareness. But she did her work well. The next morning the turtle was gone and, except for my markers, the site looked not a whit different from the soil around it.

During the weeks that followed we walked by the turtle nest many, many times, and it was never disturbed. No raccoon or opossum, no dog, no fox, no skunk dug up the nest for a feast of eggs.

These box turtles, so well fortified when they are seven- or eight-year-old adults, are virtually unprotected as youngsters, and they spend the first five or six summers of their lives creeping about in the shelter of low-growing vines and tumbled grasses. Their shells are soft for a long, long time, and the hinge of the plastron is not fully workable until they are almost five years old. They are practically naked to their enemies during the long years of their youth.

From the middle of August until October when the corn was cut and my markers were knocked helter-skelter, we visited the nest site every day. During that time, baby turtles, not much larger than a nickel, should have dug their way to the surface. If any did, I never found one, and they left the ground unstirred behind them.

The Brief Saga of
a Great Green Crayfish

T he first time I saw the great green crayfish she was drifting down the creek with a pink-and-white grubworm pinched in her left claw. She swung across the current, settled onto a stone in the gentle ripples at its edge, raised the worm to her mouthparts, and began to eat.

Almost immediately five small brown crayfish lined up in front of her, just an inch or two away, antennae waving, stalked eyes following every motion she made. First one and then another of these small watchers rushed toward the worm in the big pincer, grabbing for it with tiny claws. Each time, with a lightning motion I could scarcely follow, the great green crayfish swung her treasure out of reach and sent the little fellows sprawling with an outward sweep of her other claw.

She was so much larger than her adversaries that she should have held them off, scarce noticing, but after each sortie she became more excited and ate more rapidly, and crumbs of her food began to break off and drift downstream behind her.

Yet the little ones were unaware of this. They continued to harass her from a head-on position until she became so excited she tore wildly at the worm, shredding it, and a full half of her remaining portion went drifting away on the lazy ripples. She did seem, then, to pay closer attention to the food she still held. When she had eaten it all, she carefully cleaned the pincer that had held it and made a claw-waving rush at her hungry gallery that sent the little brown crayfish flashing off backwards through the water.

The great green crayfish now crossed the creek, walking on the bottom, creeping low among the stones and the pebbles. Just once, the current caught her and turned her on her side. She flipped her abdomen to right herself, and I saw a flash of round orange beads and knew, with a certain excitement, that she carried a clutch of eggs glued to her swimmerets beneath her abdomen.

She moved, then, among the cavern mouths at the bottom of the curved bank, crept through a flattened doorway under a ledge, and disappeared into its watery maze.

I caught only fleeting glimpses of her in the weeks that followed, for the instant she saw me or knew, somehow, that I was there, she made one powerful downward stroke with her abdomen and tail and shot backwards through the water like a meteor across the sky, to disappear into one or another of the dark caverns in the bank. Perhaps she felt the aggression in me, for I did intend to net her, just for a moment, to see the tiny transparent youngsters which should now be clinging to her swimmerets in place of the orange eggs.

But catching her had become so hopeless I abandoned the idea and practically forgot about her until, one June morning, I wandered through the pasturelands and found myself on the low edge of the creek across from the ledged and caverned bank.

And there, in four inches of quiet water, much absorbed with a small shapeless cloud in front of her, stood the great green crayfish. I leaned closer to see what the cloud could be, and she vanished with her usual reverse darting-away.

At the same instant the cloud exploded into a swarm of the tiniest crayfish I have ever seen, all backing off in every direction, bringing down their tails and leaping away in a series of graceful, swift, up-and-down arcs in the water. One by one they gave up their efforts at flight and dropped to the bottom and hid themselves in the silt.

One baby dropped directly beside my boot. He was less than half an inch long—tail, miniature pincers, and all—possibly one-eighth inch wide, pale tan, and not altogether transparent. He tried two more tiny, backward, cricket-like leaps, then he, too, crept beneath the silt. The great mother crayfish must just have removed her young from her swimmerets. Perhaps she had not quite finished when I alarmed her.

I did not see her again for nearly a week, but that broad S-curve in the creek teemed with crayfish of all sizes. Raccoons fished there nightly, leaving their tracks on the sandbars and the empty forms of eaten crayfish half-floating in the water.

Late one afternoon I saw the great green crayfish backing out from beneath a broken stone that lay in the creek several inches from the bank. Her elbows were curved upward to top-of-head level, her claws pulled back beneath her chin, and I saw that she carried a load of mud and small pebbles caught between pincers and beak.

She stopped abruptly when she saw me and I expected her to vanish on the instant. Instead, she stood still and watched me for a long minute; then, with a figurative shrug of her shoulders, she went on with her work, carrying her load downstream several inches beyond the stone and dumping it into the current.

To return to her work she had to walk toward me and I thought she would not, but after a momentary pause she came back to the stone and crept beneath it. Small whirlings of mud curled out into the water as she shovelled deeper. Then out she came with another load of debris caught between pincers and beak.

Another load and another load and another load, all of it dumped into the current at the same spot until, after emptying an unusually large load, she crept once more beneath the stone and settled quietly in her newly excavated home.

That very night, in the pale shadow cast by the moonlight at the curve of the creek, two baby raccoons sat side by side on the sandbar, their little round bottoms making the indentations in the soft sand that I would see in the first light of the morning. Their mother stood in the moving water, her arm plunged almost to her shoulder beneath the stone. Her sensitive fingers probed the hollow there and closed over the polished thorax of a crayfish.

Overturning the stone, the raccoon pulled her struggling victim into the open water. She used her two hands to pull the great green crayfish apart and to divide its portions between her bright-eyed, chirping youngsters. Then, turning only from her waist, she probed the dusky corridors of the high clay bank beside her.

Some Water Birds at the Pond

Towering clouds promised rain, and the earth lay quiet and waiting. I splashed through the marsh below the pond without stirring a frog, and followed my own foot-tramped path through the jungle of elderberry and Joe Pye weed to the top of the earth dam without flushing even a sparrow.

The dark waters of the pond, lumpy with massed green skeins of algae, stretched out before me, quiet and unbroken. Life teemed and seethed in its depths, but its surface was rippled only by the currents of its flow from inlet creek to outlet drain. No horn-jawed turtle poked its head above the waters. No foraging muskrat cleaved the surface. Not a fish leaped to a fly, nor did a kingfisher dive for a fish.

Halfway along its eastern banks I spied a hunched dark bird whose yellow legs ended, without feet, at the water line. A green heron. As I watched, he jabbed at something in the water, then raised his head, and, I presume, swallowed a small catch. That matter attended to, he leaped into the air with a squawk of belated protest, and flapped, with folded neck and trailing feet, to the upper end of the pond to continue his fishing in the shallows at the sandbars.

Close to the sandbars, at the muddy entrance of the inlet creek, a great blue heron stood in the greenish space between its grass-hung banks and speared again and again and again into its waters. I could see the white flash of his face each time he jabbed, and I wondered if he was feasting on a school of tiny fish, or a swarm of fat tadpoles, or if he was cutting to bite-size a fish or a frog too large to swallow in one gulp.

This pond, roughly rectangular, covers nearly three acres of what once was mainly marshland, and even a great blue heron's activities are not readily observed at this greatest distance across it—from corner of earth dam to corner of inlet creek.

Binoculars would help, but they hang uncomfortably on my neck and are an unmitigated nuisance when I leap a creek, crawl under a fence, or climb into a tree for one reason or another. I've carried them only twice in my years of rambling these particular fields, and scarcely more than that in my entire life. What I see, I see with my naked eye, and I usually manage to get close enough to see with certainty. If not, I don't record it.

One afternoon I slid, flat on my stomach, more than half the length of this pond in order to pry into the doings of a great blue heron who was fishing ten feet from the bank, but this morning I dropped to a comfortable seat on the earthdam, behind a thin screen of wild garlic, and watched the play from the balcony.

A pair of wild mallards materialized from the shadows under the bank not far from the great blue heron and paddled slowly between the sandbars, stopping to preen a wing here, a tail there, but mostly stretching their necks and shoveling into the soft, silted sides of the bars.

Fascinated by all the activity near the inlet, I forgot to continue my scanning of the banks, and, when at last I did, I discovered an American bittern at rigid attention, bill reaching for the sky, standing against the clay bank about forty feet across the water from where I sat.

All this time he had been frozen while I sat comfortably with my knees drawn up to my chin, my arms clasped around them, only my eyes in motion; but at the moment I spotted the bittern my left shoulder began to cramp. I fought against moving. I hoped the bittern would forget me (not very likely) and go back to his fishing so that I might watch him from this most advantageous position. I tried to contain my pain, to ignore it, but it grew intense. I slowly relaxed the clasping of my hands, eased them to the ground, carefully changed my position all around.

The bittern remained stiffly frozen; the two herons either did not see me or chose not to be bothered; but the two mallards caught the movement, and they, having moved out onto a sandbar, stood staring down the pond.

I returned to Yoga-stillness, and, after long minutes, the mallards began again to feed. They slipped back into the water, floated around the sandbar, paddled into the mouth of the inlet creek, and stopped under the pointed bill of the great blue heron.

The heron had been leaning forward, bill at the ready, staring into the water. Now he gave way to the mallards, slowly lifted his head on his long neck and tilted his body back into the grasses behind him.

The mallards, apparently, found the spot as profitable as the heron had been finding it, and they remained there, shoveling, standing on their heads, paddling around in small circles, working in that spot for what seemed to me and, I'm sure, to the heron, an unconscionably long time.

Eventually, though, they circled back into the pond and the heron stood straight on his dark legs again and resumed his fishing. But he had made only one strike when the mallards paddled back under his bill once more. The great blue heron raised his head, tilted his body back into the grasses . . . waited . . . waited. Then, lifting his long legs high, he stepped over the ducks and walked away around the bend, up the inlet creek.

As I turned my attention back to the bittern, a barn swallow came sweeping over the bank, missing the bittern's skyward-pointing bill by an inch, and neither of them flicked a feather.

A spotted sandpiper flew low across the water so that I looked down upon the white-embroidered surface of his downward-pointing wings. He landed on a knobby island of algae directly in front of the bittern without disturbing the bittern's composure. The little sandpiper walked about on the algae, picking sharply at its surface, flickering his wings as he teetered lightly over thin stretches in the green gelatin. Then he, too, flew off to the sandbars.

Only the bittern and I remained, staring remotely past one another.

The skies grew darker. A rush of gray rain came beating in from the west. The green heron slipped into the shelter of a blackberry bush overhanging the water, and the mallards vanished behind a curtain of down-curving grasses. I abandoned my post on the earthdam and left the bittern to abandon or hold at his pleasure.

An Evening of Primroses

The sunset blaze melted from the August sky. All that remained of its splendor was a sea of soft amethyst above the hills and a puff of flamingo feathers loosely afloat near its shores.

Alone in the evening dusk, I followed a path that the foxes take, through late summer grasses and patches of milkweeds all leaning askew, until I stood in a forest of evening primroses.

Six feet tall, as heavily stemmed and as stiffly branched as young fruit trees, the pale green primrose plants stretched for twenty feet on either side of me and for several hundred feet down the hilly field left fallow for the second summer.

The forest was not, at this moment, beautiful, for the time of evening blossoming had not arrived. Hundreds of faded flowers from last night's bloom hung limp and twisted from their ripening bases or lay untidily angled upon the green lances of the leaves where they had fallen. But more hundreds, perhaps thousands, of buds were swelling visibly all through the forest, their bud coverings straining against the pressures of surging flowers within.

On some evenings the primroses begin to open as soon as the sun disappears, but on others not a petal stirs until true darkness has settled. I suspect that, with primroses as with fireflies, there is a critical moment when light and temperature and humidity reach an interacting balance and the evening's activity may begin. But that moment was not yet; the invisible signal had not been given; and I waited and watched.

And I listened, too, for field crickets in infinite numbers were fiddling energetically in the thickening dusk; a wood thrush sang a haunting good-night somewhere behind the dogwoods; and a half-dozen chimney swifts twittered companionably as they captured a bed-time snack above the open field.

Slowly the darkness deepened. A lone katydid struck up

a rasping, one-sided argument in a wild grape vine at the edge of the woods. Two leather-winged bats darted erratically through the air just below tree-top level. A primrose bud directly before my eyes silently split its green sides, showing yellow-silk petals through the rents; but shreds of thickened green held across the openings and the flower within waited and gathered its strength.

At my shoulder another bud-cover split its sides and a yellow blossom popped out unfurling itself as it came. It snapped its calyces into place, flounced its four petals, wafted a faint lemony sweetness into the air, and settled itself to face the night veiled in cobwebby strands of golden pollen. Another blossom, higher than my head, popped into bloom. Then another a little further away. And then another. But the green threads still bound the straining bud-cover directly in front of me.

Fireflies now began to drift across the field drawing lines of yellow light above the grasses. A mosquito whined about my ears. A gray-winged sphinx moth, a tomato sphinx, its abdomen spotted yellow as the primroses, busied itself about the new blossoms, drinking with stiffly held proboscis from the fresh-filled nectar cups.

It approached the breaking bud in front of me, attracted by the thin lines of yellow showing through or, perhaps, by the thin line of scent that was probably escaping. Just then the green threads finally gave way and the flower popped into bloom. The sphinx moth backed off a few inches and hovered there until the final flounce of petals announced the blossom's readiness to receive visitors; then, with proboscis already golden from the pollen of other flowers, he pushed through the powdered veil of the newest one and drank the freshest nectar of the night.

The earth dropped into positive darkness. A host of disputative katydids argued with deep conviction and no evidence from hidden positions in trees and bushes. The barred owl began his nightly calling from the blackness of the pines. His hooting was plaintive to my ears, for since February he has called alone and never another owl has answered him. But two little screech owls in the oak woods quavered sweetly and cosily to one another, and the myriads of crickets never paused for rest. Neither did the mosquitoes. I kept brushing them from my face, my neck, my arms.

Down in the meadow a pair of red foxes raced close on the heels of a hapless rabbit, and I followed the course of their chase by the sound of the quick, flat yappings of the pursuers.

Now, like corn in a popper, the yellow flowers in the primrose forest and the yellow stars in the night-dark sky began popping into the world. Here. There. Right. Left. Up. Down. And all I could see was the lightness of flowers and the brightness of fireflies and stars. And, now and again, the silhouette of a dark sphinx moth hovering before a yellow blossom. Three pale-winged, pale-bodied sphinx moths (probably willow- or poplar-sphinxes) drifted from blossom to blossom and these I could see, close by, in the darkness.

Now the larger, higher-flying fireflies began to take over the evening, careening high above the grasses and up among the tree tops, flashing their long dashes or their dit-dit-dit-dit-dahs in greenish light, while the yellow lights of the earlier fireflies gradually subsided and disappeared.

Little furry creatures—meadow mice or shrews or voles—rustled about in the grasses and old leaves upon the ground, either unaware or unconcerned that I was there. Katydids and crickets rasped and fiddled. The three owls hooted and screeched. Foxes barked, primroses popped, stars twinkled and fireflies flashed. But not all of these wonders together could drown out the whining of the mosquitoes about my ears nor ease the torments of their needles upon my skin. Before these invisible attackers I beat a headlong retreat, running home in the darkness, stumbling through the ripening grasses and the haphazard milkweeds on the narrow path the foxes made.

By the Light of a Mushroom

$\mathcal{E}$very year as late summer sweeps into autumn, the ripening woods and fields break out in an extravagant rash of mushrooms, many of them poisonous, some of them deadly, and a surprising number safely edible, even delicious.

I had no intention of widening my food base among the fungi; but I wanted to know the names, at least, of those I was meeting every day. So, one blue September morning, I seated myself on the cushiony spread of dry needles in a pine grove and attempted to identify a pair of reddish-tinted, yellow mushrooms growing on the ground.

The field guide I was using lists mushrooms by habitats, a most helpful feature, but in checking those listed as growing "Under Conifers" I found myself so intrigued by the description of the mushroom *Panus stipticus*, that I set off in search of it at once and did not identify those yellow-reds until weeks later.

Not that it took me that long to find *Panus*. I found it that very day, to my dazed surprise, for I had little reason to expect it here. The field guide simply states that *Panus stipticus* grows on "old logs, stumps, branches, etc.," but it added, as an afterthought, one sentence that sent me questing through the woods as earnestly as though I sought the Grail. "A luminescent form grows in this country," it simply and broadly states. Not in some far-off, tropical rain-forest of Burma or Sumatra, but here, it said, "in this country"—maybe in Maryland?

I began by inspecting every decaying branch under the pines and finding nothing but hard gray bracket fungi or a spreading fungal whiteness. Fortunately, the book did not limit *Panus stipticus* to a coniferous forest. It noted, in parentheses, "Grows also in deciduous woods."

So I climbed the stony knoll above the pines, tramping through a small forest of bracken already collapsed on itself, and over fresh green club mosses that carpeted wide spaces of the stony ground. Tiny mushrooms grew through the mosses—in cerise and coral and white, and in pale pinks and beiges—one here, two there, sparking the green-brown earth; but nowhere, not on any of the decaying branches or rotting limbs scattered beneath the purpling dogwoods and the small, still-green oaks, could I find a single specimen of *Panus stipticus,* astringent mushroom.

On the far side of the knoll I slid down a gravelly path; traversed a veritable village of groundhog holes; passed through a rainbow of sumac trees; and entered a climax forest of oak and hickory with its scattering of maples and ironwoods, wild-cherries and sour gum, sassafras and tulip trees.

Here, among a multitude of earth-based mushrooms in a crazy quilt of dull-bright colors, lay a spreading jumble of fallen branches and limbs and logs and stumps in varying stages of decay, some half-hidden by the beaten leaves of last year's fall, others lightly dusted over by this year's early deposit of living reds and yellows. How could I possibly find a half-inch, kidney-shaped, side-stemmed, cinnamon-colored mushroom in all this jungle of possibilities?

I thought of marking the woods off on some sort of grid pattern, but on this sunlit, autumn-turning day, with hickory nuts and acorns plopping all around me, with woodpeckers drumming and gray squirrels chattering from the tree tops, with blue jays flashing their feathers and screaming lustily, I could do nothing so mathematically contrived. I struck off diagonally under the trees, moving at random, examining pieces of fallen wood as I came to them.

Many stumps and limbs were literally covered with fantastic growths of orange or yellow or rusty red. Others were crowded with gray or brown or grayish-white, either growing flat against the rotting wood or angled out from it like whatnot shelves for tiny curios. Branches far and wide produced thin, leathery brackets zoned in curving lines of browns and grays. All were speckled, pocked or overgrown with fungus specimens big and little, bright and dull, but not one growth could fit the book-description of the tiny mushroom I sought.

All morning I wandered the sun-spattered woods, not

finding the thing I looked for, but finding more centipedes, salamanders and spiders, not to mention mushrooms, than I'd found in months before—and so many of them distressingly unknown to me.

Nearly noon and time to turn indoors. I lifted a yard-long section of a wildcherry limb from its self-formed bed in the leaves, and, on its underside—not cinnamon-colored but faintly rosy buff—were whole clusters of kidney-shaped mushrooms, barely half an inch across, with bran-like scales dusted over their convex tops. Their infinitesimal stems were frosted, and they grew to one side, almost on the rims. Their tawny gills were close and fine. Like tiny, perfect, cupped shells the mushrooms rose one above the other in curving pyramids of growth against the thin black bark of the decaying limb. It was, beyond doubt, *Panus stipticus*—but was it *forma luminescens*?

I carried the fragile limb with its tiny treasures to the edge of the woods, close to the house, and left it there, for the afternoon, in its proper habitat.

That night, while the barred owl hooted from the white oaks and the little wild mice skittered through the leaves all about me, I lifted the *Panus*-clustered limb again and saw those tiny mushrooms gleam with a yellow-green light in the darkness of the September woods. The little cupped shells, so delicately lovely in the bright light of day, now shone with a magical light of their own, not simply outlining themselves, but beaming a green radiance out into the cricket-filled darkness.

So this lovely, luminous mushroom does grow in Maryland. Not overly common, not excessively rare. I found a half-dozen more troves before the season was over, and I replaced each branch, each limb, carefully, exactly where I found it—an evanescent treasure to be wistfully cherished.

The Great Mechanical Wheel Bug

T he first time I saw a great black wheel bug lumbering across a cluster of Concords I could swear I heard the clanking protest of long-unused machinery. And the last time I saw one, which was just a week ago, and every time in the years between, I experienced the same sensation of hearing the sound of rusting metal in creaking motion.

It's the ponderous, robot way they move; the cobwebbed and rusted black chitin they wear; the incredible black cogwheel that protrudes from their backs. All of it produces the inescapable illusion of unoiled, mechanical sound and motion.

They are large, too. An adult female wheel bug is one and one-half inches long from the front of her head to the tip of her abdomen. Add one-quarter inch for a short, thin, business-like proboscis, and over an inch for a pair of jointed, rust-and-gray antennae. Her flattened abdomen is deeply dished, and, measured across the concavity, is seven-sixteenths of an inch wide. (All these measurements hand-made by me.) A pair of black, silky, seldom-used wings is folded into her dished abdomen, and impossibly, and for no known reason, from the center of her thorax (between her shoulder blades) rises a hard, black, three-sixteenths-of-an-inch cogwheel all properly geared and toothed. This uncommon body is swayingly suspended from six long, rusty legs whose slow-motion knees are bent well above the level of her back.

Don't let her appearance repel you. Look—these are the only things I've ever seen her eat: aphids, slugs, Japanese beetles, green tomato worms! Now, isn't she lovely?

Actually, she doesn't "eat," she "imbibes." She captures her dinner by impaling it upon her proboscis and injecting a chemical poison. This turns her victim into a bag of juices from which she drinks as she carries it about on her uplifted proboscis.

When the emptied skin collapses upon itself she scrapes it off against a plant stem and methodically stakes out her next victim.

Because of her sharp proboscis and the chemical substance at her command, she is capable of inflicting a painful bite upon a human being, but unless she is captured or mishandled, she does not do so. She runs away instead.

Because her head is so small, only one-sixteenth of an inch wide and one-quarter inch long, I am always surprised at her alertness. I know, intellectually, that her nerve centers are not in her head, that her ganglia are scattered throughout her large body; but I don't know it instinctively, so that each time she sidles away from me into hiding, I glance at that scrap-of-wire head and wonder how she can possibly be so aware.

Male wheel bugs, of course, behave in exactly the same manner and look exactly the same except that their dimensions are smaller; but I have only once, through all these years of chance observations, seen one which I was certain was a male. This was late on a September evening when, pulling king-size weeds from the overgrown asparagus bed, I inadvertently interrupted a courting couple, separating them and dumping them both upon the ground.

Six pairs of rusty legs waved in slow-motion pandemonium until they were both upright again, then the female started away at a great rate. The male, seemingly befuddled, struggled haphazardly after her. She had some difficulty in climbing upon a tomato vine where it mingled with the asparagus and the male caught up with her. He succeeded in wrapping one front leg around her rear leg, but she brushed him off and stalked on among the jungle-mix of leaves while he stood on the ground and hopelessly waved his antennae.

Since I had unintentionally interfered with nature in the first place, I had no misgivings about intentionally interfering now. I held the female immobile and moved the male forward to touch her. He immediately attempted to clamber aboard, but she stalked away as though he were not there. His head (or rather, his ganglia) clearer now, he promptly overtook her and clasped one of her legs in the knee-bend of his and brushed another leg across her abdomen.

She stopped then, stood stock-still in the middle of her headlong rush, and he moved along her side, rubbed his head against hers, then came back brushing his legs and body against her as he came. But the moment he climbed upon her back she was off again, struggling up and down tomato leaves, striding along broad stems, burdened with the male, a clinging and frustrated passenger. The last I saw of them, darkness was crowding in and they were still heading west through the tomato patch.

Three weeks later, on an October morning, I found a female wheel bug depositing her eggs, one by one, in a small concavity of a stone on the vertical, northeast side of a wall, only four feet up from the ground. The day was dark and drizzly and the air temperature was sixty-five degrees, not the kind of day I would have expected her to choose for egg-laying, but perhaps she had no choice.

When I found her she had already laid about forty eggs in two rows tightly fitted against one another. Each cylindrical egg was one-eighth of an inch long and one thirty-second of an inch across, black with a hint of rusty-orange. Each cylinder stood on end and was sealed across the top with a small flat seal like the bottom of a shotgun shell. In fact, the rows of eggs looked like Lilliputian shotgun shells minus the brass firing ends.

As I watched, the wheel bug moved her swollen gray-black abdomen along the row of already-placed eggs and paused directly beyond the one last laid. Her cloaca slowly opened, extruded an egg, placed it exactly on end, exactly pressing against the completed row above it, and exactly pressing against the last-laid egg beside it. Her abdomen rose, her cloaca pulsed open and shut, open and shut, then remained closed for ninety seconds.

She lowered her abdomen to the last-laid egg, seemed to decide that was enough for that row, and slowly swung to the left, just touching the tops of the bottom row of eggs, until she reached its extreme left edge. Now, again, the cloaca opened, an egg was extruded and placed below the first one in the second row, exactly fitting against it. The abdomen rose. The cloaca pulsed. She waited two minutes before she lowered her abdomen again, opened her cloaca, placed another egg, second in the row and exactly touching the one above and the one beside it.

Only half a minute and she placed the next egg, fifteen seconds and she placed the next, three minutes until the next.

It was four hours later when she left her almost circular stand of eggs and, with flattened abdomen and closed cloaca, settled to grooming herself for another hour. She roamed about within a dozen or fifteen feet of her one hundred fifty eggs for seven days, then wandered off along the wall into a frosty October night, and I never saw her again.

I felt a deep gratitude toward that wheel bug and a rising excitement each time I looked at the egg-filled concavity. Next spring, for the first time, I will discover what a wheel bug looks like as a baby.

More Mushroom that Glows

Because so many readers wrote letters or called me asking for further information on "the mushroom that glows," and because the month of November is still prime time for mushroom hunting, let me assure you that I did find the mushroom, and that it did, indeed, shine in the darkness with a positive green glow.

Nothing that I write is contrived. Everything I write happened to me or before my eyes and is as true as wide-ranging study and a lifetime of loving observation can make it.

I do use field guides, as I have freely stated—and a whole library of other books besides. I make no pretense of knowing all about nature or of having all her secrets at my fingertips; and, since even Roger Tory Peterson carries—and uses—his own field guides, I count it no disgrace. In this instance, moreover, the field guides mentioned *Panus stipticus* only sketchily, and I could find nothing about it in other literature.

Where I walk there are no paths. Much of the terrain is clear, but almost daily I climb over or among fallen trees, work my way through underbrush, slide on my stomach beneath barbed wire and electric fences, and, from July until winter, push through goldenrod, milkweed, ragweed, elderberry and what-have-you higher than my head, or walk in creeks because their overgrown banks are impassable.

What I am pleased to call "my territory" is roughly one square mile in extent and is comprised of the marshes, pastures, fallow fields, and woodlands of eight separate but contiguous farms whose owners have given me the deeply appreciated privilege of walking upon their lands at all hours, in all weather, and in all seasons.

And that is exactly what I do. I spend at least one hour each day in the field, usually average two, but have spent as many as six. On some days I may walk five miles and on others scarcely stray from my dooryard. It all depends on what attracts my attention, where, and how soon. My goings and comings are extremely erratic—I may be out as early as four o'clock in the morning and as late as ten o'clock at night, but that last is a rare occurrence indeed.

For all these most obvious reasons, and for others less apparent, walking with me is best done vicariously and from the warm, dry comfort of your armchair.

Please accept my assurance that the mushroom *Panus stipticus forma luminescens* does grow in Maryland, that I found it within twenty-five miles of the center of Baltimore City, that it is probably to be found in any of the public parks in this radius, and, I have no doubt, in wooded areas over most of the United States.

But the fact that they do grow here is no guarantee that you, or I, will find them on any particular outing or even on any particular search for them. I did, to my utter astonishment, find them on the first morning I actually searched (September 17, 1973, to be exact), but I spent five consecutive hours of concentrated looking in an area I know most thoroughly, and I had abandoned the hunt for that day when I found them.

And, yes, I did find six more separate growths of this luminescent mushroom before their season was over, which means that from September through December I found seven specimens, and I walked, and looked, every day, although I never again specifically sought *Panus*. Discoveries and experiences in nature, I have learned, usually come when one walks with every sense alert but with the self submerged in the living- ness of all the earth around. Even in my intense search for this mushroom I found it only after I had turned away from the hunt.

But the mere fact that you, or I, found *Panus stipticus* last year does not mean that we will therefore find it this year or next. It does not, apparently, grow a second time on the dead branches which once it graced so beautifully. On all those seven limbs or branches on which I found *Panus* last year not one specimen is showing this season. As a matter of fact, I have not yet found, this fall, a single mushroom of the species.

But in spite of its elusiveness the glowing mushroom is well worth hunting for. Its form is so dainty, so entrancingly lovely, it would be worth seeing even if it did not shine in the darkness. It is not a bracket fungus, nor does it spread flatly and tightly to the wood surface. It is not papery, nor leathery, nor striped in any manner.

I have tried to think what it is like and the nearest comparison I can make, with any satisfaction to myself, is to a freshly dried apricot-half. It is somewhat of that shape, of that thickness, of that texture, even of that color, but not twisted nor wrinkled. It is gently curved, like a little cupped shell. It is small, scarcely half an inch in diameter. Its outer surface is lightly dusted with scales, as though a fleck or two of wheat germ had been scattered upon it. Its interior is hung with intricate rows of self-color gills like silken flower petals, and this whole lovely thing is held upon a frosted pedestal of a stem, placed well to one side and possibly one-eighth of an inch high.

It grows in clusters, in curving pyramids, upon dead and decaying branches on the forest floor, not piled one upon the other but growing separately and distinctly in pyramidal rows upon the branch.

And it grows predominantly hidden from sight. I tell you this most hesitantly and reluctantly—it grows mostly on the undersides of those decaying limbs and branches. The upper reaches of the pyramidal clusters are usually above the levels of the surrounding fallen leaves, but the heavier growth is almost always hidden from view, the gilled interiors growing against the earth.

As the golfer is asked to replace his divots, so the walker in the wilds is asked to replace the stones he turns over and the branches and limbs he picks up. And so I plead with you, if you go looking for the mushroom that glows, that you replace, exactly in position, every branch or limb you raise in your search. For it is always, summer or winter, the roof of somebody's home; and, in this season, some small hibernator, perhaps a spring peeper, is depending to some extent upon the insulation of that branch to see him through the desolation of winter. He lies in a state so close to death that the slightest alteration in his surroundings may make his return to life impossible.

To see a branchful of these mushrooms glowing softly in the darkness of an autumn woods is an almost spiritual experience that I sincerely hope each one of you may have—but please put them back where you found them.

Low Bird at the Feeding Station

Among the gratifying numbers and variety of December birds who flock to the spread feast of fine-cracked corn and sunflower seeds under the lilacs, at the edge of the woods, is a little brown pair who are alternately scolded and ignored by their feathered kinsmen, and roundly scorned by most human watchers who happen to recognize their species.

The two birds don't mind at all being on the bottom rung in the pecking order. They come flitting in together, morning and evening—more often if the day is stormy—and settle close to the bare stems of the bushes, away from the bombastic jays and the sharp-billed woodpeckers. They scratch the earth and peck single-mindedly among the bits of grain they turn up until the curve of their little crops can be seen under the fluff of their breast feathers. Then they fly off to the fallow fields to put a proper topping of wild weed seeds on their effete meal of domestic, broken corn. But if winter dusk is gathering or the weather is wild, they dispense with the weed seeds, fill up on the corn, and fly without guilt back to the close shelter of the pines below the hill.

The first time I saw them they came flying in through a slanting mist of wet snow, dropped down beside the busy feet of a male towhee, and began at once to eat the grain he had just scratched out of the cold cover. The towhee cocked his head at the rude table guests and moved away with a jaunty air to scratch in another place.

After that initial gaffe the newcomers did their own scratching, not, I think, because they learned better manners or felt any shame, but simply because there was plenty of food and not, actually, much need to scratch.

When they first flew in, hungry and a little beaten by the weather, they both appeared unkempt little hoboes, but as they settled down to the spread food and their empty crops began to reach a comfortable distension, they smoothed their feathers and took on a look of greater respectability.

True, the female of the pair looked a pleasant, frumpy character in feathers of dingy brown and mousey gray. Even the light line at her eye and the bars in her wings were dull and indistinct, as though she had been distracted and hadn't quite bothered to complete her costume.

But the male was a natty fellow. There was nothing unfinished or neglected-looking about his attire. The top of his head was a deep ash gray, his cheeks were snowy white, his chin, his throat, his upper breast a glossy black. His eye-line, too, started out a glossy black but it changed to chestnut just past his eye and spread over the nape of his neck, across his back, and over his fine-formed wings. His back and shoulders were longitudinally striped in black, his underparts were pale gray-white, and his wing-bars were as white as his cheek patches and delicately stitched with a fine black border.

It was the little female who had led the way through the storm to the spread feast at the edge of the woods, the little female who dropped beside the towhee scratchings and stole the first bit of tempting corn from beneath his feet. But now it was the male who suddenly felt territorial, felt the instinctive need to protect his food supply against all comers. He left off his hurried, greedy feeding and came at his mate on mincing feet with his dark bill clicking, his body crouched, his black throat puffed, and his wings and tail spread to their widest stretch of grayed and chestnut feathers.

Instantly, the female dropped her dowdiness and stood, neck stretched and body trim, staring him down and moving not a fraction of an inch. Slowly, the male simmered down, smoothed his feathers, and went back to his feeding; but he could not resist, now and then, in the pause between a scratch and a peck, the spreading of a wing, the puffing of his throat. But at each slightest gesture of threat his mate assumed her uncompromising stance and he quickly dropped his histrionics and turned his attention back to the cracked corn at his feet.

Two juncos, following their own whims and paying no

attention to the other birds about them, fed closer and closer to the newcomers. Suddenly the natty male turned upon them the full threat of his fuming advance and spread war regalia. The trim gray birds moved an inch out of his way and went on with their feeding. He came at them again, from the opposite direction, and they moved just enough to let him pass by. When he came at them the third time their moving revealed a male downy crouched over a sunflower seed just beyond them, and the little brown bully continued his advance right up to the busy woodpecker who merely raised his head and, without uttering a sound, delivered several sharp, lightning-swift stabs to the newcomer's unprotected gray head.

Subdued and hurting, the erstwhile disturber-of-the-peace stood with drooping head while his mate and all the assorted winter birds went on with their pecking and scratching and their contentment-while-eating sounds without the slightest interest in his mishap.

After what seemed to me a long time, and probably when his wounded head had stopped hurting, he moved back beside his mate and ate quietly until she flew off toward the pines through the slanting mist of snow, and he flew meekly behind her.

And he continues to follow her. They feed at the station every day—the only pair of their kind—eating quietly together, never quarreling with each other, nor, from that first day, ever threatening a bird of another species.

The male still comes at his mate on mincing feet, his dark bill open, his body crouched, his black throat puffed, his vocal cords producing strange noises, and his wings and tail spread to their widest glory of grayed and chestnut feathers. But there is now a subtle difference, an air of courtship, even in December; and his mate's attitude seems to carry less rebuff and more tolerance for the little showoff.

They are as pleasant a pair of house (English) sparrows as anyone could hope to entertain at his winter feeding station.

A Meadow Full of Meadow Mice

I f I gave a thought, the entire summer, to the population of meadow mice (meadow voles) cowering timorously in their grassy tunnels each morning as I crossed the small grass field on my way to the marsh, the creek and the pond, I'm sure I imagined no more than three or four dozens of the little gray-brown creatures going about their invisible, ceaseless, day-and-night activities in the unused pasture.

I knew they were there, of course, widespread in the field. Once in a while, curious about my unseen neighbors, I would spread the long grasses apart with my hands and find a mouse-wide pathway cut trimly through the heavy cover, and, once or twice, several little pathways radiating out from a small round hole in the ground.

Then came early winter when a light tracking snow on the ground made me revise my estimates upward by several dozen meadow mice, for their tiny, scurrying tracks laced and inter-laced the filmy covering on either side of the diagonal path I took across the field. But even one mouse can leave a great many tracks behind him in the course of a night's racing about, and the sum of the tracks of a dozen mice could be fantastic.

That winter was a snowy one and the white covering of the field grew deep and hard-packed, but the meadow mice lived just as comfortably and much more safely under the snow as under the leaning grasses, traveling their winter-locked home-land in meandering, white-domed tunnels, earthen-floored, and just exactly meadow-mouse-sized.

Only rarely, now, the two-two track of a meadow mouse appeared in a fluffy surface of new snow or the frosty surface of the old. What wild daring, what surging call to adventure, what claustrophobic intensity drove an occasional mouse to tunnel his way up to the open air, to scramble out upon the roof of the world where his dark little body became immediately so dangerously and so individually visible? There were tracks of dogs and foxes and skunks and cats and pheasants and crows on the snow, and there were hawks watching from the skies by day, and owls by night; and often and often the little wild skein of meadow mouse tracks ended in a small red spot and a brushing of feathers or a deep-set pouncing of paws.

But most of the meadow mice, with their tiny dark eyes and their small round ears snuggled close to their heads, stayed in their snow-arched tunnels nibbling at weed seeds, nibbling at grass blades, enlarging their burrows, enlarging their families, and, for the most part, deftly evading the teeth of any predator hungry enough to dig down through the snow.

So that when, at the very end of January, a warm south wind melted the snows down to a mere skim of white over the field, the little arched tunnel roofs melted quickly away and revealed to my startled gaze a network of squiggly, earth-bottomed runways veining the remaining snow in so criss-crossed and close-placed a pattern that I knew it must have taken a thousand mice to keep so vast a food-finding communication grid open through the piling up of snows.

But I was wrong. Authorities tell me that a modest estimate of the meadow mouse population would be eight hundred per acre, or about twenty-five hundred meadow mice loosely and comfortably scattered about in that three-acre field.

Authorities also modestly estimate that twenty-five hundred meadow mice will eat fifteen hundred pounds of food each month. In this unused field that meant fifteen hundred pounds of weed seeds, roots and grasses; and yet, unless I went to some lengths to uncover their cleared-by-eating runways, their depredations were almost as invisible as the little mice themselves.

Of course, now that the covering snow was gone, with the long grasses still flattened to earth and every narrow mouse-trail exposed to view—well, there were a great many mouse-trails. . . .

Among those myriad trails and runways, I found, when I searched, only half a dozen little grass huts, and all of these were clustered at the foot of a slight northerly slope where the shielded snows lingered longer. This was interesting because in real snow country that is the way the meadow mice live.

These nests were small rounded domes built of dried grass blades and stems all cut into lengths that varied little from being exactly one inch long. In the center of each dome was a small room, and its only entrance was a neat round hole on one side at ground level.

In the underground burrows the nest is furnished with a warm lining of soft, dried grasses, while the rest of the burrow, unlined, is made up of store rooms and toilet rooms with galleries between which may open, probably accidentally, into galleries constructed by other meadow mouse families.

For meadow mice are gregarious, and, while they would not tolerate a strange mouse in their private rooms, the runways, whether under grass or under snow, seem to be freeways upon which all who wish may scamper and all who wish may gather unstored food.

Not that they are immune to the nervous stresses and strains of overpopulation. They belong to the same family as the lemmings and share with them their rich fecundity plus the resulting madness of massed migrations and the physical succumbing to physical diseases for non-physical reasons.

A little female meadow mouse bears her first litter of pink, blind babies before she is three months old and she may have more than a dozen litters in a year. As few as three and as many as ten little mice may arrive at each birthing, but the usual number is probably five. (There were, in fact, three litters in the several grassy nests I found when the snow melted—six wee pink mice in one and five in each of the other two.)

Authorities estimate, again, perhaps, modestly, that, under ideal conditions, the mating of one pair of meadow mice on January 1, could easily result in a *million* meadow mice, all alive and still bearing, on December 31, twelve months later. This is theoretical, of course. No laboratory has either the space or the motivation for pursuing such an experiment to its conclusive hordes; and, in nature, these ideal conditions do not exist.

Nevertheless, in some years, in some locations, natural

conditions come close enough to the ideal to produce so many thousands of mice to the acre that they become as much a plague to the meadow mouse clan as to the earth they devastate, and vast migrations are undertaken.

This small grass field has gone unused for several seasons and, now, when I part the clumps of winter grasses I find runways three-mice-wide and only about one-mouse apart, and I sometimes wonder if some morning I may find stampeding meadow mice piled up by their thousands in the narrow, steep-banked creek at the foot of the hill.

Those Who Hide Away

For months, ever since the salmon-toned leaves fell from the sassafras sapling in the fencerow below the house, I had been keeping an eye on a brownish silk cocoon in which the pupating body of a Promethea moth was spending the winter.

The silken fabric of this cocoon enveloped one mitten-shaped leaf at the tip of a twig on the sapling, rolling it inward, using it for a base of construction and as additional insulation from the drying winter winds. The leaf did not fall to the ground, in spite of the extra weight swinging upon it, because several strong twists of cocoon silk were looped about the leaf stem and the twig from which it hung.

The cocoon's thick brown bulk swung, prominently visible, on the tip of the thin green branch. It bounced and swayed with every breeze and streamed out flat on the fury of the winter winds. Its weather-proof fabric turned the winds, endured the hail, and shed the rains, though sometimes it shone with an icy overcoat or sagged dully under a whimsical cap of mounded snow.

And then, on a February day, when not a breeze stirred in the fencerow and the cocoon hung dull and still in the gray gloom of snow-heavy clouds overhead, its drooping thickness aroused the curiosity of a blue jay who had passed it by, half a dozen times a day, for twenty weeks or more.

I saw him hesitate in mid flight as he went by, turn, swing back, and alight on the slender branch which nearly toppled him as it dropped under his weight. Keeping his precarious balance, tail up, tail down, he peered at the cocoon with one dark eye and then the other. He pecked tentatively and inconclusively at the elastic covering, then, giving it up, flew off into the oak woods.

But half an hour later he was back, probing heavily at the silken hammock while his insecure perch bobbed up and down.

Probably a dozen times during that gray February day the blue jay returned to worry at the fine webbing of the cocoon, and, just as the setting sun broke briefly through a gap in the cloud cover, flooding the bleak world with a golden stream, I saw the blue jay peck rapidly at the cocoon, then stop, cock his head, and peer down at it. Now he reached carefully, tail up, branch sinking, pushing his beak deeply into the cocoon. He pulled his head back, too quickly, lost his balance, and fell. His flailing wings caught the air just before he touched the ground and he beat his way upward at a long slant into the woods. And in his black bill he carried a prize.

I was out, just then, to scatter an evening bird-snack under the lilacs at the edge of the woods, and I walked down to the fencerow to verify what I knew had happened. I found the bruised and battered cocoon with a three-cornered snag in its outer covering and a deep puncture wound reaching into its middle, into a smooth oval cavity in the padded silk where only a few moments ago a living, dark shelled pupa had lain. The Promethea moth, helplessly encased in its silken vault, had lost its life to the determined bill of a gourmand bird.

Winter living is a precarious venture, even for those who hide away.

Last fall half a dozen adult mourning cloak butterflies crept behind the loose bark on a stump in the woods. Now on a February night, when they are deep in hibernating torpor, a foraging skunk pulls away that bark and daintily devours the morsels he finds. As he nibbles each dark body he drops the wings, like dry, thin flakes, from his lips to the leaves at his feet.

And so it goes. A raccoon, digging under a log for over-wintering grubs, unearths a hibernating chorus frog and enriches his diet with its sleeping flesh. A deer mouse, hunting over the woods floor, finds a papery cocoon among the curled hickory leaves. He bites through its thinnest end and finds the fat pupa of a luna moth a fine delicacy for a mouse's stomach.

His cousin, a white-footed mouse, spends the winter in a country garage. He dines one day on the black-worm bodies of three woolly bear caterpillars who were sheltering in the warm protection of their own rich fur, curled down among empty sacks in a cupboard there.

Sharp-billed chickadees and titmice search the vines and the bushes, the briar patches and the evergreeens. They drive an opening wedge through the dried-foam doorway of every praying mantis egg-case they can find, and they cheerfully swallow every egg the mantis so laboriously emplaced.

Red-bellied woodpeckers and golden-winged flickers chip away the pottery walls of the mud wasps' organ-pipes and enjoy the edible treasures of wasp grubs and preserved spider-bodies hidden within.

Sparrows and finches, chickadees and titmice practice the same tactics on the hordes of spiderlings that swarm inside the silk-blanketed balls swinging in tattered webs in protected angles of buildings, posts and outcroppings. They do the same thing to the tougher, jug-shaped sacs the Argiope spiders leave behind.

Last February, heavy rains flooded the marshes, swelled the creek over its banks, and flattened every reed, brier and herb to the ground. I had watched, in the fall, a black-and-yellow Argiope finish off her egg-case under the top leaves of a purpled blackberry stem at the creek's edge. Now I found this stem, with egg-case still intact, bent low, and hanging into the creek with flood waters pouring over it.

Wading into the overflow of rushing waters, I succeeded in lifting the entire bush from the water, turning its top in the opposite direction so that the egg-sac was out of the flood although it hung at a drunken angle from its few remaining guy lines.

A few days later, after a fresh deluge, I found the bush torn from its roots and the still-clinging egg-sac buried under a thin cover of silt and sand. I dug it out, moved it away from the creek, and braced it upright among some honeysuckle; only to find it, next evening, trodden underfoot by a herd of young cattle. The egg-sac was sadly misshapen, but untorn and still recognizable.

Hoping that a few young spiders might still be alive, and thinking that I might watch them come out in the spring, I brought the egg-sac home and tied it to a rose bush outside my window.

Two days later—proof that at least a few spiderlings had survived their ordeals by water and by cattle—a Carolina wren punctured the sac, consumed its inhabitants, and left the empty relic to dangle in the February wind.

Snakes in the Grass — and the Window Well

The moist earth under the clutter of brown leaves in my window wells still feels miserably cold to my ungloved hands. But the March sun, shining through the leafless trees, has warmed it enough to set blood coursing in cool bodies and awaken the chorus frogs and the spring peepers who have hibernated there. I have already lifted several of the early risers from their self-chosen prisons, have carried them down to the pasture fence and sent them off toward the wild, wet freedom of their ancestral marshes.

It is still too early for the vari-colored and vari-sized toads to appear in the wells, and I thought it was too early for the garter snake, too. But this morning when I scooped a little black-throated male peeper from the top of the leaves I saw the head of a tiny garter snake peering out from the narrow earth-seam between house wall and metal well-guard. Its head appeared far too large to come through that space, and the earth in which it was embedded looked uncomfortably dry and hard, but I know from past experience that I shall find the little snake among the leaves in a day or two. I shall lift it out and set it free in the garden where it will, I hope, work with me against the hordes of slugs marauding there.

Funny about these garter snakes who hibernate in my window well. Every spring there is only one, at least I find only one, and always it is in the most northerly of the east-facing wells. Perhaps the snakes are capable of climbing out of the twenty-inch deep, straight-sided well on their own, and so I do not see them all, but none that I have seen has been making much progress in its straining, curlycueing attempts to get itself out of that confining, half-mooned space, walled in by metal and glass.

For the first several springs of my residence here the snakes I rescued were adult size, growing, in that time, from eighteen to thirty inches long. I always assumed, in the absence of any real way to know, that it was the same snake returning year after year to the safe hibernatorium it had once fallen into by blunder.

But these past three springs the only snake has been a slender little thing, pencil-slim, and looking far too delicate to survive in a world that contains a fair share of hawks and crows and foxes and cats. The first spring it was only seven or eight inches long. Last spring it measured closer to ten inches, and, judging by the size of the head I saw this morning, I imagine it will be a twelve-to-fourteen inch snake I will lift to freedom a few days from now. But whether it is the same snake that wintered here last year I do not know.

Last March on a 45-degree day, under a brilliant sun but with a cold wind blowing, I found two garter snakes intertwined and lying, stiff as cardboard, on the grassy bank of a stream. They were eighteen and twenty inches long, and their inert bodies were sleeked with a thin coat of dried mud, as though they had pushed themselves through a moist layer of thawing earth into open air that was less warm than their hibernation headquarters had been.

Two hours later, with the sun dropping behind the hills and the thermometer plunging into the thirties, the two snakes were still lying in the same position, obviously incapable of movement. I covered them with handfuls of dried grass. Early the next morning the grass was scattered and the snakes were nowhere in sight. I suspect that they were already being transmuted into the warm-blooded flesh of a furry mammal who had dined on them during the night.

Garter snakes—and this includes those trimmest, slimmest members of the family, the ribbon snakes—are the most commonly seen snakes in this area, although they are not always recognized. Their background colors as well as their markings are extremely variable. The bodies may be striped or spotted, and the colors may range from black through shades of brown and green to olive. Even the three yellowish stripes—one down the middle of the back and one on each side—which normally distinguish the members of this tribe, may be brownish or greenish or bluish or whitish, or even invaded by other body markings.

These snakes are so commonly seen because they live in such varied locations—from marshes and hillsides and fields and woodlands, to gardens and lawns and even city parks. The one vital requirement, other than a minimum of cover, seems to be a supply of moisture or, at least, a dampness in the earth.

For garter snakes are closely related to water snakes, and I occasionally see them swimming in the quiet edges of the pond, their heads held curved well above the water surface and their bodies undulating in a side-to-side motion that is really beautiful to see, especially when two of them are swimming together.

They mate in late spring and give live birth to twenty or thirty little six-inch snakes, most often in August. Each baby snake appears singly from under its mother's uplifted tail. It is coiled tightly in a clear "cellophane" membrane through which it soon thrusts its head and glides out into the big, wide world. If they are not disturbed, they may all lie there beside their mother for an hour or more. When they disperse, each little snake will go off on its own, perfectly capable of locating its own food—earthworms, slugs, leeches, baby mice, baby fish, baby frogs. Garter snakes are probably the last snakes to go into hibernation, so their young have two or possibly three months in which to eat, and grow, and learn to (or fail to) evade their hosts of predators.

Against these predators they are not completely defenseless. They can, of course, hide themselves well in grass and in leaves; but they can also strike and bite vigorously, and thrash their tails about, and they can exude an odorous musk from glands at the base of their tails. How effective these measures are for tiny, newborn snakes I do not know, but, depending on the size and courage of the predator, they sometimes work for older ones, and they have to learn to use these defenses when they are small.

Once I rescued an adult garter snake that was wandering around in the lawn grasses ahead of a mower, and took it to

safety at the edge of the woods. Garter snakes are not poisonous, but they can inflict painful bites, so I picked this one up by
holding it directly behind the head, and, to avoid its flailing
twenty-inch body, I held it out at arm's length. I knew about
the musk glands, but I could scarcely credit the copious amounts
of unpleasant-smelling, whitish fluid the snake threw about.

Incidentally, snakes are not slimy. Their bodies feel cool
and dry to the touch, like soft, well-tanned leather. They are
wild animals, free in their own environment, different on many
counts, but not to be despised for all of that.

Hot as a Flicker's Nest

Along the western slopes of the Allegheny mountains, in years past, when any countryman spoke of a grossly overheated area, whether heated by stove or sun, he used the ultimate simile to describe it: "It's hot as a flicker's nest in there!"

How hot, I wondered every time I heard the expression, can a flicker's nest be? It became a childhood ambition to put my hand into a flicker's nest to learn for myself just how excessive the heat was in there. But the few flicker nests I ever discovered were high up in great old trees whose lowest limbs were well beyond my reach, and, though I did some energetic climbing in nearby trees, I never quite managed to get close enough to a nest to test its temperature.

Thus, on a certain April morning when I caught the glint of golden underwings from a mated pair of flickers, I watched with more than casual interest. They were hunting a nesting site among the trees on either side of the shallow creek in my neighbor's marsh. Perhaps, after all these years, a nest might be located low enough so that, with thermometer in hand, I could find out exactly how hot "as hot as a flicker's nest" is.

The two birds investigated every knot hole and hollow and tapped exploratory bills along a hundred interesting limbs and trunks without finding exactly what they wanted. The mustachioed male did cut a few whopping chips from the wildcherry tree on the high bank, making the black bark and the light inner wood fly in all directions, but the female flew at him with scolding cries until he left off his sculpting and followed her on an inspection tour of the sassafras grove on the top of the hill.

From the sassafras grove they flew to the oak and hickory woods that stretched across the lower end of the small valley, searched it for a day and a half, then worked their way back up the marsh until they reached an ancient willow just below the pond in the middle of the valley. And here they stopped. Only eight feet up on the rough-barked trunk they immediately chipped out a circle nearly three inches across and chiseled a hole three or four inches deep straight back from the opening.

Only eight feet up! I could scarcely wait for their nesting to begin. But, after that enterprising opening, the birds suddenly became indolent. They flew about the marsh and the pond on no errands whatever, or sat, tail-braced, on the trunks of neighboring trees and filled the April air with their wickering. Then they found an ant hill in the fence corner across the marsh and spent long hours sprawling about on the great crumbly mound, occasionally tucking black-and-red ants under their wings, and constantly thrusting their sticky tongues into the ant hill openings to collect mouthfuls of plump, lemon-flavored ants. And nearly a week went by before the nesting hole was completed.

But when it was done it was a beautifully carved-out cylinder in the heart of the willow trunk. A dark cell nearly eighteen inches deep and more than six inches across, it had a round doorway already polished by their comings and goings. Inside, a few wood chips and a sprinkling of sawdust on the floor made it comfortable for the brooding flickers and their eventual babies. The grasses at the foot of the willow were thickly littered with untidy scatterings of large-chiseled wood chips and rough-powdered sawdust.

Finally, quite early on an April morning, when the countryside was shrouded in fog and a fine drizzle fell through it, the female flicker entered her new willow-wood home and settled herself to produce her first egg. The male pecked around at the bark of the nearby mulberry trees, eating a few insect eggs or new-hatched grubs to pass the time. Every so often he flew over to perch in the willow tree and to talk softly to his mate hidden away inside the trunk.

It was well past the middle of the morning and the mist still fell softly through the gray fog. Suddenly, the valley was filled with vivid streaks of light flashing up, flashing down, from a blazing, quivering nucleus of light high up in the fog, while the air tightened, then rocked apart with intense explosive sound. The willow tree split from top to bottom, through the middle of its giant trunk, right through the middle of the new flicker nest. The scorched limbs and charred branches flew through the air, scattering for hundreds of feet along the creek bank and out into the marsh.

The male disappeared never to be seen again, nor any trace of him found. His mate still sat on the gray ashes of the wood chips on the bottom of one-half of her cylindrical nest, her feathers vanished, her brick-red flesh baked dry to her bones.

In the earlier hours of that morning I stood near the willow watching the course of the flicker's nesting, but at the moment of violence I was nearly half a mile away, just opening the back door of my home. I felt the strange sensation which I can only call a "tightening" of the air, saw the wild leapings of light, was enveloped in the unbelievable force of the explosive sound.

And all that day and all that night the fog and the fine drizzle continued, but there was not another flash of light, not another burst of sound, not even a quiet rumble. It is possible, I suppose, that, just as in a winter snow a charge of electricity is sometimes generated to be discharged in a surprising flash of lightning and resultant thunder, so, possibly, a charge was built up in the constant-drizzle-through-the-fog to be discharged dramatically on that April day.

One wonders, of course, why in that particular spot? Why that particular willow tree? Did the hollow within that tree, heated by that little flicker body, have anything to do with the electrical attraction? Whatever the reason, one thing I know beyond doubt—for one catastrophic instant that was surely the hottest flicker's nest ever to be known or imagined.

When Blossoms Are Kings

The liveliest spot I know on a bright May morning is an old apple orchard at the height of its bloom. Its unpruned branches trail into weedy aisles a-reel with color, and fragrance, and flavor, and texture, and motion, and sound. One walks in fragrance so heady one tastes it and color so vital it rings in the ears.

Dark trunks; green leaves; rosy buds; pale blossoms; and massed, curling threads of pollen-dusted stamens where a million translucent honey bees tumble and roll and saturate the air with a low, warm humming.

Sunlight flashes on hard-working wings: robins and swallows and thrashers and towhees building or brooding or tending their nestlings. Bluebirds and house wrens, flickers and starlings dart in and out of their knotholes and hollows. Catbirds and cardinals and little striped song sparrows steal about in the raspberry tangles.

Wiggly-nosed cottontails skitter from forms in high-tufted grasses and zigzag away beneath the low branches. Grizzled brown groundhogs scoot down to safe darkness, then turn and waddle out to sit on their door mounds and to whistle alarms at my crossings and turnings. And a white-tailed deer, a hornless one with dainty feet, springs down the aisles on a magical path of grass-topped trampolines.

A fall of faded petals trails in her wake, for first bloom is over and the single, first-blooming blossom at the tip of each cluster has, hopefully, been pollinated; its fragrance has vanished, and its now useless petals sift haltingly down into the tangled grasses and brambles.

This is the time of second blooming. Two blossoms, now, at the base of each cluster are opened wide, spilling their new fragrance into the slow stirring air while the two or three buds in the middle, flushed with rosy babyhood, are swelling and pushing toward their own nuptials only a few days away. The orchard actually blooms more fully in its third blooming but, by then, so many faded blossoms hang in each cluster that its glory is veiled and misted over.

Nearly three weeks of bloom, nearly 100,000 blossoms on every full-grown tree, but every pink blossom does not turn into a little green apple. Nature is prodigal but rarely foolhardy. She is heedless and wasteful of individual blossoms but she carefully tends the whole species.

A full crop of 100,000 apples in one season would deplete the mother tree so that it would never be capable of bearing again. In fact, the weight alone of such a crop would bring the tree crashing to the ground long before its apples could ripen.

Nature's system of checks and balances is elaborate and intricate beyond any governmental schemes, but in its round-about reachings it does manage to work. By natural processes of natural laws, less than five percent of a tree's blossoms become juicy autumn fruits.

An apple blossom has a female pistil and twenty male stamens but neither the blossom nor the variety is self-fruitful. Other blossoms of other varieties must be close by or there can be no fertilization. In every pistil there is an enzyme that is an invincible warrior against "self" so that any blossom dusted with its own variety of pollen simply dies and is dropped from the tree. Thus millions of blossoms are summarily disposed of.

And that's not all. Although the blossoms remain open and fragrant for two days, or even for five, depending on the weather, their stamens suffuse themselves in pollen during only one three- to four-hour period of that time. No wonder the bees, on this sunny, almost breezeless day, are so rollicking, so intoxicated, so tumbling-about in the powdery pollen. For—although I'm sure the bees are not thinking of this—if the weather were cold, or the winds were strong, or the rains poured down, they would not or could not leave their hives. The honey bees would miss their pollen harvest and the apple blossoms would miss their pollination. But, of course, those baby buds developing in the middle of the blossom cluster would give the tree still another chance to produce apples—if the weather were fine at pollen-producing time.

But it is the first-opening blossom at the tip of each cluster that is the most likely to set fruit. There are not so many of them, and they don't all open at once, so they are many times more likely to receive pollen from another variety of apple; and that pollen, fresh and plenteous, is likely to fertilize most of the tiny ovules, or seeds, deep in the base of the pistil.

Now, the more ovules developing, the more hormones produced, the greater is the supply of nutrients drawn from the tree. That physical fact gives the first blossom in every cluster a head start on its siblings that few, barring accident, can ever overcome.

Apple blossoms and so, of course, apples, are produced not on twigs (except rarely), but on short, stubby spurs that grow only about a quarter of an inch a year. During the winter there is a wooly bud at the tip of this spur, and in spring this wooly bud opens and a cluster of buds and leaves grows forth. If it is a strong spur and has several leaves it can develop more than one apple from its blossoms. Even though the center "king fruit" is absorbing most of the nutrients, side fruits can grow quite well on the lesser supplies they are able to draw, but the spur on which they grow must be strong.

If a side apple, or even the king fruit, of any cluster is undernourished, the tree discards it. Five or six weeks after the blossoming of the last buds an abscission layer forms between stem and spur and the failing fruits are dropped to the ground.

By the end of June the tree holds only six or eight percent of its once potential crop of apples, and now summer storms, insects and diseases will reduce even that number by half; so the healthy tree, with safety to its own life and the probability of a crop next year, will produce only ten to thirty bushels of, mostly, king fruit.

What of all the untold billions of wasted blossoms in all the May-time orchards blossoming on this day? Well, their disintegration enriches the soil on which they fall and they will eventually nourish more billions of blossoms, many to be identically wasted. But the revelling bees don't consider it waste, nor does the chance human being, who wanders in fragrance so sweet he can taste it and color so vital it rings in his ears.

The Hatching of the Wheel Bugs

All winter the tightly-packed round of wheel bug eggs sat as immutable and as apparently lifeless as the stone wall to which it was attached.

March warmed into April, and April into May, and still I could see no change in the eggs. They looked as much like minute, black, upsidedown shotgun shells during the first week of May as they had in the latter weeks of October, but still I kept an irregular, several-times-a-day watch over them.

One afternoon at nearly five o'clock, with the wall in deep shadow, and the temperature dropping to the mid-sixties, I saw the pale seal of one of the eggs move aside, and what looked like a buffy-yellow worm with two pin-point black dots for eyes slowly began to extrude from its egg like cookie dough from a press. The pressure seemed to come from beneath the body, pushing it up, vertically, from its shell.

Probably most insects hatch from their eggs in a worm-like larval state, so it was not surprising that the wheel bug was doing so. But when, with a lens, I examined this vertical worm, I discovered that it was actually beetle-structured, with tightly-folded legs and antennae pressed into its tender body.

The emerging buffy-yellow body began to rock back and forth as it rose, almost imperceptibly, from the shell which held it. When it had rocked itself for twenty minutes, its head, thorax, legs and antennae were out of the egg and I could see its pale-orange abdomen beginning to rise above the shell.

At that point it began to extend its legs and antennae, to work them in and out and up and down, until, at last, the tip of its abdomen sat on the lip of the eggshell. The little creature toppled to a horizontal position atop the other eggs—and it was hatched!

Now it stood all awry on its gangling legs, tried to get the hang of those useless threads, to do something about those unmanageable knees, and, after what seemed hopeless effort, finally worked its body to the proper position, swinging inside the angles of its legs, halfway between high-bent knees and microscopic feet.

Its antennae were giving trouble, too. They hung down across the black pin-points of eyes like two loose hairs, they tangled with the pair of wobbly front legs, and they made a difficult situation even tougher. But after another five minutes of concentration and practice the antennae were cocked above the eyes, the legs were acting like legs, and here was a new little wheel bug, all buffy-yellow of head, thorax, legs and antennae, pale-orange of abdomen, and without a sign of wings or of a wheel on his back.

He was just ready to step off the egg cluster when twenty or thirty pale egg seals behind him shifted to one side, and twenty or thirty buffy-yellow, worm-shaped creatures began, all at once, to rise from their shells.

Immediately the newly-hatched wheel bug moved among these hatching siblings, rubbed them with his antennae, stroked them with his front legs, busily attended them for the thirty or forty minutes it took for all of them to get free of their shells.

And while he was helping his siblings he began to change color. Gradually but perceptibly his head, thorax, legs and antennae changed from buffy-yellow to buff, to tan, to earth-brown, to chocolate-brown, to black, while his pale-orange abdomen deepened to orange, to reddish-orange, to red.

The color change took nearly two hours to complete, and, during this time, his twenty or thirty siblings learned to manage their own unmanageable legs, began to change their colors, and all of them were brushing and stroking the more and more new little creatures who kept rising from their shells.

By 10:30 that night there were fifty little wheel bugs hatched or hatching, and the temperature had dropped to fifty-two degrees. At 11 p.m. with the temperature at fifty, I went to bed and left the remaining eggs to hatch unwatched.

But no new eggs hatched in the coolness of the night, for at five a.m. there were still only fifty baby wheel bugs clustered on the stone beside the eggs, and all of them were dressed in regulation black and red.

As soon as the morning sun topped the woods and streamed its warmth onto the egg cluster, a dozen pale seals shifted and a dozen buffy-yellow heads began to rise from the black cylinders. Yesterday's hatchlings immediately converged onto the egg cluster, brushing, rubbing, stroking, assisting with the hatching of their newest siblings.

With all this assistance in the warmth of the sunlight these newcomers hatched swiftly. Before two hours had passed one hundred fifty baby wheel bugs milled stiffly about on or around the cluster of now-empty eggs. Their bodies were less than an eighth of an inch long, their thin legs were more than twice as long as their bodies, and all the legs were bent double so that the little bodies swung above the stone with their folded knee joints high above them.

Those nine hundred folded knees and three hundred long antennae gave the family an over-all hairy appearance, although they were quite smooth and not fuzzy at all.

The gathered group separated little by little during the daylight hours that followed until there may have been half an inch of space between any two of them, and they had moved perhaps two inches away from the old home cluster of eggs.

One of the youngsters—was it the first, lone-hatching one? —wandered away from the crowd. He was nearly five inches away, walking stiffly down the wall, when a hunting spider, zebra-striped and a quarter-inch long, came zigzagging behind him and seized his bright red abdomen in its fangs. The little wheel bug tried to walk away but he could not move. The spider hung on, its injected poison took effect, and the wheel bug drooped.

The spider shifted him into its front feet and bit him again on thorax and head. The little wheel bug went limp, his legs folding beneath him. The spider shifted him into its second pair of legs and with its front pair bent the wheel bug's antennae forward and back.

Apparently satisfied that its captive was unconscious, the spider then dragged him an inch or two up the stone, lifted him into the air, drank his life juices, and dropped the empty black-and-red form to the ground.

Before darkness fell the remaining wheel bugs moved back to the empty egg cluster, and there they spent the night. This became the pattern of their living for the immediate days that followed. Each day the group moved a little further from the home cluster, and each night fewer of them returned.

Several more fell victim to the hunting spider, many of them dangled loosely in the small webs of other spiders on the wall, but some, hopefully, went off to live in independent wheel bug fashion.

For nearly two weeks dwindling numbers of young wheel bugs returned to the empty egg cluster each evening, and, near the end of that time, several of them shed their first skins and left them there atop the shells.

Then came a night when not one wheel bug returned to the egg cluster. The next day I found seventeen of them standing about on an aphid-infested rose bush close to the wall. Two days later I could not find an aphid on the bush but I found seventeen young wheel bugs, looking fat and impudent, nearly twice as large as on the day of their hatching, still with brilliant red abdomens, and still without a sign of a wing or a cogwheel on any of them.

The Lantern-Bearers

*J*une is the month of moonlight and roses, of butterflies and honeysuckle, of new-mown hay and wild strawberries, of emptying nests and filling ponds and mid-summer's night, and fireflies.

Fireflies usually appear the first evenings of the month by handsful, a few nights later by bushels, and in mid-month by shimmering clouds that fill the air with their dancing lights.

On any given evening the first lights may twinkle soon after sundown, or darkness may deepen into night before the earliest fireflies shine, for their beetle libidos are released not just by shadow, but by interacting stages of temperature and dampness, too.

As these several atmospheric variables approach the proper proportions to one another, the early-evening fireflies stir from their resting places and, at the biologically correct moment, their frail bodies rise up from the grasses in curving "J's" of yellow light. An adventurous one here, a second one to follow, half a dozen there, an upward falling of sparkling lightdrops steadily increasing to a dazzling shower that rises, rises, yet never reaches more than three or four feet above the tops of the meadow grasses.

Not at this hour the erratic brilliance of flying sparks nor the capricious corn-in-a-popper flashing we will see later in the night. These gentle, first fireflies of the evening are the soft-bodied *Photinus pyralis* who sweep into the air with their rear segments aglow, then drift invisibly downward with tail lights extinguished. They execute a gracefully paced, on-and-off, up-and-down dancing supported on fragile wings of crinkled black chiffon, but all we see is the glow and the upward sweep of light, so the numbers of fireflies seem limitless.

For two hours, a little more, a little less, these dark fireflies sparkle and mate and dance over the dew-dampened lawns and meadows and grainfields. But even as they begin to subside into the shrubbery and the grasses, before they have doused their lights and settled for the long hours of rest ahead of them, their big, brash, hard-shelled cousins are zooming over their heads flashing long, long dashes or twinkling dit-dit-dit-dit-dahs in dazzle-lights of green and blue. These bold and hardy beetles, *Photuris pennsylvanica*, career through the air for hours, and then, near the middle of the night, gather about the leafy heads of isolated trees in glittering clusters of floating lights until the approach of dawn upsets the ratio of darkness and warmth and humidity and quiets the dancing lanterns of the night.

Why do they dance? Why do they glow?

They dance because they are adult fireflies, and it is summer time, and the air is dark and warm and moist, and they are genetically programmed to be physically active under these conditions.

They glow because, long ago, their ancestors developed bioluminescence as an incidental accessory to the system used to rid their bodies of oxygen. Later, when the primeval beetles became oxygen-using creatures, they retained their light reaction simply because it was not easily lost.

The lights are produced by an enzyme system not necessary for the life of the individual firefly but essential to the survival of the entire firefly family, because their flashing lights have become recognition signals between male and female of the several species.

Most, if not all, of those apparently random dancing lights above the summer meadows are actually males engaged in fiery courtship rituals exact in every particular. The color of the firefly's light, its brightness or dimness, the duration of each flash and the intervals between, possibly even the position and the motion of the firefly in the air are important in this twinkling dance of life.

And down in the grasses, resting on blades and stems and stalks, the female fireflies wait and watch and flash the proper responses to the coded courtship messages of the nearest airborne males.

The male of the early-evening firefly hovers low above the grasstops and gives one flash and a lingering glow of red-yellow light. Exactly two seconds later the female of his species responds with one quick flash from the grass. The male replies and the scintillating conversation continues with possibly a dozen or more males vying for the attention of the one female. When such a conversation ends in a successful mating, the female turns off her light of the night while the unrequited males (and probably the triumphant one) continue their twinkling quests.

In the large and vigorous *Photinus pennsylvanica* species the ratio of the sexes is almost exactly reversed, with about fifteen females to every male. This lopsided population statistic probably accounts for the insouciance of the males who zoom through the air flashing their greenish-blue lights like intermittent meteors.

Courtship dances, stylized or free, are fairly common among the less-conscious forms of life—insects, birds, and fish, for instance—and all of them are interesting to the human watcher who stumbles upon the show. But only the firefly puts on a gala spectacular, with thousands of featured performers, night after night after night. And few of us stay to watch.

A friend from the desert lands of southern Utah spent three summer weeks here in the east, waiting to be shipped out during the years of World War II. "I came out of the mess hall the first night," he said, "and I saw all those little lights dancing around in the air, and I never saw anything so pretty in all my life. Nobody else paid any attention to them. I asked someone what they were and he looked around and said, 'Oh, them? That's just lightning bugs!' Later someone else said they were fireflies, and I like that name better. Why, I didn't sleep for most of that three weeks just from watching those fireflies. That's still the most beautiful thing I've ever seen, and I can't understand how you easterners can just walk around and not even look at them."

"It's like sunsets," I told him. "If we only had one sunset a year . . ."

"Yeah," he said, glancing at the cerise and copper clouds transfiguring the bare rock peaks behind us, "but those fireflies are *alive!* And all those pretty lights flying about! You ought to *look* at them!"

Three Special Toads

The three toads who live in my patio flower bed probably don't rank high on the intelligence scale set up by human beings for judging their lesser travelling-companions on this planet, but I'm sure they rank well enough as toads.

The level of consciousness for the average toad is pretty dim. Its awareness does not extend much beyond the level of its own physical comfort—heat and cold, dryness and dampness, the presence of food or its absence, and the approach or disappearance of a possible enemy. But these three toads of my acquaintance, I like to think, have an added dimension of awareness—me. Not that our relationship is any great shakes as a relationship goes, but it is something more than nothing.

They see me every day through the summer months, I'm sure, while I see them less often—perhaps not more than once a week—yet each time we meet they appear to be expecting me. I pick them up and they nestle in the curve of my palm for as long as I am willing to hold them.

Their season of hibernation is long, and the dim mind of the toad would seem able to retain only instinctual memories, yet every spring when I lift these little fellows from the window well—where they have hibernated by their own illogical choice —they behave as though this is the normal method by which a toad leaves its hibernatorium. And, now that I think of it, for these three no doubt it is. I suspect that every spring of their lives (for they are very young) I have lifted them out into the world of the living; and I must, therefore, be a part of their instinctual knowledge.

Toads have a selection of several defense mechanisms. They can hop away; they can burrow rapidly, backwards, into cover; they can "play dead"; they can void a copious urine; and they can exude a poisonous mucous from the glands on the tops of their heads—but this, so far as I know, only from outside pressure, such as being grabbed by a cat or a dog. But not once has any of these three toads been even slightly defensive with me.

Just this morning I lifted the largest toad from a window well—I don't know whether she fell in or leaped in after the several moths and mosquitoes which fluttered around the lighted basement window last night—and she behaved exactly as though she expected me to rescue her. She sat quietly on the window sill and allowed my hand to close around her. She hung loosely in my grasp without a quiver of either body or legs until I brought her to patio level, and she snuggled down comfortably when I cupped her cold body in my two warm hands and carried her to the moist-earthed flower bed at its side.

I don't like to use the word "snuggle" to describe the way she settled into my palm—there is something not quite the same as when I rescue a warm-blooded, furry, baby rabbit from one of the cats and it snuggles into the secure dark warmth of my hands—but the toad seemed to feel secure, too, in her dim, cold-blooded, amphibian way, and she did not leap away when I released her, but sat back between palm and thumb and rested there quite unconcerned with leaving. I had to push her off into the clumps of fragrant lavender in order to go on about my own affairs.

I refer with feminine pronouns to this largest of the three toads because she has, I think, reached maturity, and the granular skin beneath her chin remains the same light color as her breast. Male toads darken under their chins as they reach maturity and their backs are not nearly as bright and colorful as those of the females. The back of this largest toad is clear and bright. Its dorsal folds sparkle with glints of gold and the tips of its warts with amber and red. She grows broad and squat and low to the ground, a really promising beauty.

The two smaller toads are still quite unidentifiable, except as toads. They still wear nondescript mottled browns or gray-greens, and their bodies retain a younger, more frog-like slenderness, although they must be two inches long.

Toads do not mature until they are four or five years old, and they may live for as long as thirty. These two small toads are probably three years old and the large one close to five.

So far as I know, none of them has yet made a return journey to native pond or puddle, but the largest may possibly have gone this year. I saw her often during May, even into its last week, but not again until this morning, so she may have answered the sweet crooning song of the males at the pond and gone off on a June bridal journey. This is not late for toad nuptials. Male toads remain singing at the ponds from early spring into July, while the parade of paramours comes and goes.

A female toad lays her eggs, like strings of dark beads, in long, continuous, coiling strands of jelly into shallow water at the pond's edge. There are from four thousand to twelve thousand eggs in the clutch of an American toad, and, in warm weather, they will hatch in as short a time as four days. Through June and July these shallow waters teem with wriggling hosts of tiny black tadpoles.

As soon as these tadpoles have turned into toads and have completely resorbed their tails (when they are four to six weeks old), they are ready to leave the pond; and they do so in armies of delicate, fragile-legged bits of life seeming completely inadequate to deal with the rough, eat-or-be-eaten etiquette of the marshes and the fields.

And they are inadequate. They are gobbled by the hundreds by crows and blackbirds, by chickens and ducks, by turtles and snakes; but those who manage to survive this banqueting mayhem for just two weeks are half an inch long, appear much sturdier, and have grown as fat as little toads should be.

Toads keep growing all their lives, moulting their skins over and over again to accommodate the new size. Male toads usually don't exceed three and one half inches in length, but females are sometimes larger, and the fat bottoms of both sexes seem to just spread and spread.

I suspect that "my" largest toad looked so bright and colorful this morning because she had just changed into a new skin. I wish I had caught her at it, for this is an interesting process, hard to see. Her skin is continuous inside her mouth, and she just starts at the two corners of her lips and sucks her whole coat off, swallowing it as she goes.

Nursery Days of
the Giant Fishing Spider

The marsh was an August tangle of gold and purple, scarlet and white, with boneset and lobelia, with asters and Joe Pye, with sunflowers and goldenrod; and the warm, bright air of the rain-washed morning was redolent with late-summer fragrance.

At a curve of the creek I paused in the shade of a slender willow and listened to the gurgling of dark, knee-deep waters, to the rumbling drone of bumblebees in the jewel weed blossoms, to the wickering of flickers in the oak woods, and to the idiot calls of cuckoos from the thickets on the hill.

I looked across to the opposite bank for a remembered mixture of meadow beauties and heal-all, but I forgot the flowers the instant I saw, instead, a lacy white dome of spider silk that swirled together several top leaves of a Joe Pye weed whose roots probed the muddy margin of the creek and whose top reached barely a foot above bank level.

I waded the pebbly shallows above the curve and came up, still in spicy willow shade, beside the silken nursery a-sparkle with droplets from last night's left-over rain.

Through the lacy gauze of the nursery walls I could see a tiny ball of almost colorless, almost unseeable, baby spiders clinging, not to each other, but to the silken lines with which the nursery was threaded. They hung close to the nursery roof under the overhanging shelter of a Joe Pye leaf. Directly beside them, glued to the underside of the same leaf, hung the white, silk-parchment egg sac from which they had all escaped. The bottom of the sac was spread raggedly open and bits of fluff from its interior hung scattered in the silken lines beneath so that the sac looked as though it had exploded the spiderlings into the nursery.

I knew little about fishing spiders right then so I did not expect to find the mother spider still in attendance, nor have any idea she would be so large—and I gasped when I saw the great dark spider outspread upon the leaves below the nursery web. She stretched a generous four inches from tip of front foot to tip of hind one, and her velvety gray-green-brown body in the center of that hairy rosette of stalwart legs was more than an inch long and at least half that wide at the broadest part of her cephalo-thorax. She was, in other words, a bit broader at the shoulders than at the hips.

With her eight legs all spread-eagled she was much larger than my palm. I brought my hand close beside her, trying to get an idea of her actual size, and she dropped like an agile pebble to the next level of leaves. There, with her legs curved beneath her, she still looked extraordinarily large but no longer spectacular. When I attempted again to measure her she darted back to her original stand.

No lethargy there. She was nimble and swift and intensely aware of every movement in her surroundings. She seemed eminently capable of driving off any spider or predatory insect which might attempt to take her young, and of frightening away any small bird with the same idea.

I think she never left her post. No matter when I visited the nursery she was there. She never dropped into the water beneath her when I approached, as members of her species are supposed to do, and, as the days went by, she ceased to show any alarm at my visits—or any interest, either.

I could find little information about her in my books, but I did identify her as a Giant Fishing Spider of the genus *Dolomedes*, probably *tenebrosus*. She is capable of running about on the water surface or of diving beneath it, though I never saw her do either; and she is known to feed on small fish or tadpoles, but it is likely that she more usually eats insects.

She carries her large white egg sac about in her mandibles from the time she constructs it until the eggs hatch and the little spiders, living for a while inside the sac, are ready to force their way out. Then she glues the sac to the leaf of a plant overhanging the water and spins a roomy six-by-eight-inch nursery all about it with silken strands in a lacy weave.

I don't know for how long she carries her eggs, perhaps for as long as three or four weeks. I feel certain that she does not eat during this time, for, creature-memories being what they are, if she laid her egg sac down long enough to capture a meal she would not likely remember to take it up again.

But no such accident had befallen this mother. Her egg sac had been safely hung and its multitude of tiny inhabitants were now out in the wider world of the nursery web where they grew darker and faintly larger with every passing day. I suppose they fed upon one another as all baby spiders are said to do, for there was no other food in evidence and they were unquestionably growing.

Every day, after the first, when I came to that curve in the creek I found the little spiders scattered through the nursery and oblivious of my presence.

But on the eighth day I found them clustered in a loose galaxy under the Joe Pye leaf. Close together, but not touching, they hung at ease on their silken lines inside their gossamer house, each one a little dark star with eight pale legs, like rays, surrounding it. As I bent over their nest they were startled, and each one moved a leg, or three or four, and it was like a thousand dull little stars twinkling in their small galaxy. This was the first time they had shown any awareness of the world beyond their nursery, so I kept testing them, moving my arms, nodding my head, and at every motion the galaxy twinkled—and stayed exactly in place.

On the ninth and tenth days the little spiders were gathered into a tight burry ball, but as I leaned over them they sprang apart, forming again the loose-clustered galaxy.

And on the eleventh morning I sat on the creek bank and watched with the dark spider mother while her several hundreds of sons and daughters went out into the great, wide world to seek their fortunes.

The departing adventurers clambered down the silken stairs by twos, by threes, by groups of ten, each tiny dark body hurrying away on the twinkling rays of its eight fine legs. And when the youngsters reached the ends of those filmy strands they wandered off among the leaves of the Joe Pye weed in which their nursery was hung, or they swung down into the watery wilderness of the jewel weeds on silvery threads of their own manufacture.

And that, I thought, was that.

The Aberration of a Giant Fishing Spider

When her several hundred sons and daughters left the nursery web, I expected the spider mother to follow quickly, returning with arachnid inscrutability to her child-free life of walking upon the water, of stalking tiny fish and water-dwelling or waterside insects, of dropping to the creek-bottom with crystal air bubbles caught in the hairs of her body; but she sat, immobile, on the outside curve of the empty nursery, her eight long legs spread in a wide rosette and her great body pressed flat against the gossamer construction.

For more than two hours I waited in that place of sunlight and shadow—not idly, for I was exploring by sight, sound and smell, the subtle nuances that made this first day of September so much more autumnal than the latter days of August—and in all that time the mother spider did not, so far as I could tell, blink a beady eye or move a single hair.

The next morning, out of habit well-established in the last dozen days, I stopped by to check on the empty nursery. I was sure that the mother spider, her duties done, would be gone from the scene, but still, I looked for her. And found her, to my intense surprise, outspread on the underside of the Joe Pye leaf just outside the base of the nursery web, her favorite guard post during the eleven days of her hatchlings' dependency.

On the second, third and fourth mornings—and I began to visit her in the evenings, too—I found the spider mother in exactly the same position on exactly the same Joe Pye leaf. What was wrong with her? Could she be guarding phantom youngsters in a real nursery? Could an instinct-managed creature develop a mental aberration, or a spider get a kink in its nervous system? I thought not and decided she was physically ill, probably dying now instead of waiting and wandering until the inevitable freezing death of winter.

But, on the morning of the sixth day after her youngsters had gone, I found my giant fishing spider, my *Dolomedes tenebrosus,* sitting one leaf-whorl below her usual post on the Joe Pye weed. Incredibly, she carried in her mandibles the empty, dried and darkened egg sac which she had somehow removed from the nursery.

After a few moments of glinty-eyed waiting the giant spider mother dropped down to a lower leaf-whorl, then further down to another, and I watched in disbelief as she went off among the jewel weeds with the old egg sac clutched tightly in her mandibles.

I examined the empty nursery. The leaf to which the egg sac had been glued showed a dark stain where the egg sac had hung, and a hairline tear, but that was all. The lacy nursery was neither torn nor damaged.

It so happened that in the last few days before the spiderlings left the nursery web under the willows I found three more webs of the same kind along the upper reaches of this narrow stream. Each filmy balloon-shaped nursery had a host of tiny, pale, almost invisible baby spiders clinging to the silken filaments inside, and each had a great, dark mother spider on lurking guard outside among the leaves of the tickseed sunflowers and the jewel weeds where the nursery webs were hung.

But there was one difference between these nurseries and the one under the willows. These three new mother spiders all plummeted like stones into the water beneath them every time I came near—just as the textbooks said they would—and it was only by the grace of a thirty-eight degree morning when their cold-blooded bodies were too sluggish to move that I was able to identify them positively as belonging to the same species as my Number One *Dolomedes* who had never once leaped into the water at my approach.

Now I watched the three new nursery webs with avid interest. As the days went by the little spider bodies in them darkened and grew fractionally larger as the weakest babes provided the food upon which the stronger ones grew stronger.

There came a day when I found the spiderlings in each nursery web gathering into a galaxy of their own, just as the little spiders in the Number One nursery had done, and, like

them, these babies were suddenly aware of my approach, twin-kling their fine, light-colored legs at every motion I made. Their mothers, as always when I came near, plummeted into the water from their guard posts at the base of the nursery webs.

Two days after their first awareness of me, these little spiders left their nests, dropping down the wispy threads and disappearing into the bronzing leaves on the water's edge where they would manage, some of them, to live through the winter, to grow prodigiously, and to become next summer's velvety dark, startlingly giant, fishing spiders.

Within two hours after the last straggling youngster had departed the nursery, each dark spider mother dropped from her guard station, and from my sight, into her own earth-and-water living for whatever weeks remained to her.

Now four empty and forgotten nursery webs flashed silver-white in vagrant currents of air along the meanderings of the creek between pond and woodland; but darkening, drying egg sacs hung in only three of them.

Number One nursery web held only a dark-stained Joe Pye leaf and my frankly bemused ponderings on the instinctual pro-gramming of a certain giant fishing spider.

The Rehabilitation
of a Battered Sapsucker

With a squealing cry and a flash of dull crimson a male sapsucker undulated across the back corner of the yard and dropped into the untended thicket at the base of the telephone pole. His eight long toes had scarcely grasped a supporting branch in the tangle of dogwood and pokeweed before he wrenched a pokeberry from the purpled raceme that dangled before his face, swallowed it and pulled another.

One after another he ate the dark berries, snatching them wildly, until his distended crop stood out like a small balloon. Then, right there on the exposed branch, he settled his breast feathers over his feet, pulled up his eyelids, and he slept.

His sleep, I soon saw, was not a simple catnap after lunch. It was the stupor, the almost comatose state, of utter exhaustion from which he barely roused at long intervals, ate another berry, and sank back into his torpor.

Even allowing for the rumpled conditions of sleep, he looked a mess. His feathers were disarrayed, not quite clean, coming apart at the barbs, and their colors were faded and dull.

How this sapsucker could be so battered, so starved and exhausted, in a storm-free, berry-and-insect-rich October I do not understand. Unless, perhaps, he had blundered into a seldom-used building and had, at last, been rescued, or perhaps, had been held captive in a chicken yard or a cage where he could not eat the grain he may have been offered. In either case, he would have spent his days flying madly about trying to escape and could have beaten himself into this condition.

However it happened, he was in sad shape; and he stayed among the pokeberries, doing nothing except eating and sleeping for two full days.

On the third day be climbed a few feet up the telephone pole, clinging to its roughness with his down-curved claws and bracing his vertical body with the spines of his tail feathers.

Turning his head from side to side, he peered at the dark wood
for moments at a time, moving upward only in short hops,
halting and hesitant. It was as though a stirring memory or a
faintly rising instinct bade him climb but did not tell him why
he climbed. Suddenly he looked up to the sky, whined faintly,
dropped back into the shelter of his berry-filled haven, and
began to feed again with graceless snatchings as he had on the
first morning of his arrival.

On the sixth afternoon he flew twenty feet across a perennial border to a peach tree that still held its deadish-green leaves,
and he climbed to its top. He even hopped flat-footedly along
two of its heavier limbs for a short way before he flew silently
back to the safety of the berry bushes.

Strangely, the current mockingbird-in-residence, a scrappy,
pugnacious individual who disputed his boundary lines several
times a day with aggressive mockingbirds on adjoining terri-
tories, and who, with flailing wings and snapping beak, drove
off any bird of any species who questioned his right to all those
berries—that same mockingbird accepted the starving, woolly-
minded sapsucker without a fuss, and seemed, even, to go out
of his way to avoid a confrontation.

On his eighth morning of convalescence, the sapsucker flew
down to the base of the peach tree. He climbed slowly, and
when about five feet above the ground he struck the thin bark
a tentative stroke, stood back, and stared at the dent he had
made. He struck again in the same spot. Stopped and stared.
Something let loose in his head then, or in his little psyche, and
he beat upon that tree with such lightning runs that his head
became a colorless blur. Fast and then slow, fast and then slow,
he drummed, and the bark and the soft inner wood flew about
him like spray in a fitful wind.

Now he stopped drumming and began to pick out the
sweet, living wood from the last squarish hole he had made. He
drilled five holes, all in a line, and then swabbed them out with
the brushy tip of his tongue. Not much sap rising, not in
October, but some still flowed, and the sapsucker mopped it
up as it slowly collected in his fresh-made taps.

While he waited for more sap to seep into his springs, the
sapsucker backed down the tree and hopped awkwardly through
the grasses to the low, crumbly rising of an ant hill. He plucked

a black ant from a grass-tangle path. The round head and abdomen protruded on either side from his narrow bill; he worked it back, turned it lengthwise, and swallowed it whole. He probed the entrances to the ant hill, ate several more unlucky inhabitants, and flew back to wipe the welling moisture from his gathering-basins in the peach trunk.

From that day, then, the sapsucker was transformed. He became again, what once he had been—a sapsucker with an identity. A sapsucker who flew confidently among the orchard trees; who chiseled holes in their trunks; who ate their cambium and drank their sap. A sapsucker who fed to satiety on deftly captured ants and caterpillars and mosquitoes. But he was still a sapsucker who fed mainly on purple pokeberries and slept, without fail, in the sheltering tangle at the base of the telephone pole.

He was, moreover, a sapsucker who began to draw the indignant attention of the Lord High Mockingbird, who now scolded at and pursued him, but not quite relentlessly, not quite continuously, and with far less than his usual vengeance. The wary sapsucker thus had only to elude the mocker's feints and manage to avoid a face-to-face encounter.

And so it continued until the fifteenth day of the sap-sucker's sojourn in our backyard.

On that morning the fully healthy sapsucker, his feathers preened properly neat and trim—the blacks glossy, the whites (especially the vertical signature splash on his dark wings) gleaming, the yellow wash on his speckled underparts aglow, and the color patches on his forehead and throat flaming like poppies—this sapsucker, on the fifteenth morning, stretched out his neck and plucked the final purple berry from the tangle of bushes.

At that instant the outraged mockingbird dropped, scream-ing, upon him from the top of the telephone pole, striking his back with nail-sharp toes, beating him about the head with well-practiced, pounding wings.

The sapsucker had eaten the last pokeberry and was ready to leave hospital anyway, so he beat an undignified retreat to the southwest woods. Presumably he continued his southward migration, for I never saw him in the area again.

A Garden of Magical Mushrooms

Once upon a November morning when the temperature hung somewhere in the upper thirties and a light dusting of frost crystals clung to goldenrod and grasses, I, with three joyously romping dogs for company, raced along a newly cleared right-of-way on the woods-bank that fringes the public road. As we ran, I noticed scattered patches of a strange new fungus growth on the bare earth among sparse clumps of bronzed and twisted curly grass.

This fungus grew somewhat in the familiar manner of earth tongues, having several "fronds" or "leaves" curving up from a common center, but, instead of being black and fleshly as earth tongues are, these were white and most delicately formed. That they were a fungus I did not doubt, for they had, quite literally, sprung up over night to stand two to four inches tall where yesterday afternoon nothing of their kind had grown.

No use to attempt an identification with three excited dogs —my own Great Pyrenees, a neighbor's Border Collie, and another neighbor's personable hound of mixed ancestry—skylarking around; so we raced on our happy way, I doing some fast and fancy side-stepping to avoid crushing the new mushrooms and the dogs seeming not to bother but not touching a single one.

An hour later, with Kela asleep in her fenced backyard and the neighbors' dogs, hopefully, dozing on their own doorsteps, I went back to the right-of-way to see what I had seen.

Although the sun shone warmly through a thin November haze, its rays did not probe the heavy ranging of the woods to the east; so the woods-bank still lay in morning shadow though the dusting of frost was gone from its grasses.

The overnight fungus still stood fresh and attractive and I bent to examine a specimen at my feet. It grew from the bare earth as a broad, somewhat angled, white base that quickly divided into several gracefully rising "leaves." These leaves, more like long, narrow straps, rose at a gentle angle to perhaps two inches from the earth at their highest point, then curved their ovalled ends downward to almost, but not quite, touch the earth again.

Each leaf was three or four inches long, from half an inch to an inch wide, each was a substantial eighth of an inch thick, yet they looked as delicate as blown-glass petals.

Every leaf was longitudinally striped, alternating white and clear, like vanilla-flavored ribbon candy. They actually had more the crystalline look of ribbon candy than the fleshy-vegetal look of mushrooms, except that their edges were frayed like the freshly torn veils of deadly amanitas. There was no veil, of course. This was not the standard mushroom form. These members of a lowly biota apparently belonged to the sac fungi, for they had neither gills nor obvious pores.

From the vantage point of an oak stump I looked up and down the woods-bank. These strange fungal forms, like lovely, stemless flowers, were randomly scattered for several hundred feet; and while most of them grew in the regular pattern of gracefully curving strap-petals like the one I had examined, some were frail stems supporting wide, dangling, free-form leaves, and others were twisted and twirled into fantastic variations of the spiralled shavings from a wood lathe. But, regardless of shape, every one had tattered edges, and every one had crystal stripings evenly spaced and sharply defined.

Kneeling, I pulled my floor model from the ground, lifting it gently, with two hands, as I would lift a puff ball ready for the skillet; and I found that, like a puff ball, its footing was firm, it resisted being pulled, and it came up from its little depression in the earth with soil clinging to the roughness of its bottom.

It felt cold to my hands, but no colder than the earth from which it came; it looked brittle, looked as though it would shiver into splintery bits at an indiscreet touch, but I was still thinking "fungus" so single-mindedly that I could not see what I was looking at.

I broke off the tip of a leaf between thumb and forefinger. Something vaguely familiar about the way it broke. . . . No skin to peel off. It was "all of a piece," its alternating white-and-clear stripings making up the whole of it. Not flaky, not dry, not jelly-like, not buttery, not leathery—and while I pondered its substance the sample vanished before my eyes and left a droplet of water between my fingertips.

And I opened my eyes, and I saw.

A whole garden of fascinating fungi, and every single specimen fashioned from ice crystals! Ice crystals growing over this whole woods-bank, growing and producing repetition after repetition of the same lovely form as though they were daisies or daffodils or dandelions or daylilies. As though someone had scattered seeds of this particular species of ice crystal along this right-of-way. As though ice crystals grew in gene-directed forms.

These were three-dimensional reproductions of individual plants from frost pictures on winter windowpanes. Distant relatives of flat fingers of first-ice creeping across the ponds. Kissing cousins of slender icy columns honeycombing loose banks of earth, and of heavy obelisks of ice thrusting upward from the roots of goldenrod in the middle of the clearing.

The southerly hanging sun swung around the end of the woods, fanned its golden warmth over the woods-bank, and this blue-jeaned amateur naturalist sat cross-legged on the earth and watched her whole garden of magic mushrooms melt, thaw, and resolve itself into a dew.

But this was a miracle to be repeated over and over on successive mornings of that particular November and in every November to follow—and, rarely, in March and April. On mornings when the thermometer rests on the frostpoint (thirty-eight degrees Fahrenheit) or a trifle below; on mornings when the humidity level is at some unknown (to me) but exactly right plateau; on mornings, moreover, which I have never been able to forecast or to pinpoint or even to guess, those lovely crystal forms appear once more on the woods-bank.

The garden grows smaller, though, with every passing year, as the spice bushes and the chinquapins and the sassafras and the pin oaks creep back over the once stripped-to-the ground right-of-way, as the bare earth and the sparse clumps of curly grass disappear, in short, as the environment changes. For even mushrooms grown from ice crystals require a proper habitat.

The Voices of the Barred Owl

Last night I awoke sitting straight up in bed as a high-pitched scream jagged the air from the edge of the woods just a few feet outside my window. The scream began piercing and high, descended slowly to a tom-cat snarl, and then dropped into a series of turkey-gobbles in the familiar voice of the barred owl.

No matter how many times I hear that demoniacal scream, at least a hundred times a year, it strikes through me (if close by) with a knife shaft of terror, swift and startling. And each time, as I subside into the comfortable knowledge that it is only the barred owl, I am acutely aware that there are other hearts out there in the frozen night pounding in mortal panic because it *is* the barred owl.

Little white-footed deer mice feeding on seeds and beetles among the leaves on the forest floor; little thick-bodied meadow mice feeding on seeds and beetles among the grasses on the lawn; little puff-feathered wintering birds with heads tucked under their wings in the sheltering green of the yews and the pines; and even the little fierce-billed screech owls sleuthing about for their own timid prey.

The barred owl is a big bird, nearly twenty-four inches long, with a spread of broad wings to twice his length, but his yellow-scaled feet are so small and weak that he must confine his hunting to creatures that are also small and weak. Quite fortunately for the barred owl, the small and the weak are usually present in excessive numbers; and since, like most predators, the barred owl eats whatever of his prey is the most plentiful, he lives mainly upon mice. In seasons of high mouse populations he will eat, I am told, more than two thousand mice per year.

I don't know why he screams as he does. It sounds, to me, like a scream of frustration, like mortal outrage with earth's arrangements, as though his crop is empty and his food impossible to come by; but I have read that predators scream—or roar or bark—in order to startle timorous prey into revealing their hiding places.

If that is the reason for the barred owl's screaming, I can see no point in his prolonging his cry beyond the first few shrieking notes, for they certainly bring every creature within hearing distance to an instant alert. By the time he has come down the scale and finished with his snarls and his varied finale, all the larger creatures have returned to their own concerns, and the tiny ones have either melted into deeper hiding or congealed into indistinguishable humps among the leaves, certainly more silent and less visible than they were before his wild voice shattered the pattering darkness.

His scream could just as well be interpreted as a yell of triumph, or a cry of repletion, or a war-whoop releasing a build-up of tension. I have no idea what his screaming means, but, for that matter, neither can I translate his hoots or his laughter, his groans or his chuckles or his snarls, or any of the other varied syllables and sounds that make up his oral vocabulary.

His signature call, which says to any human listener who is interested, "barred owl here!" is a series of eight hoots drawling downward at its end—something like: "HOO-HOO, HOO-HOO. . . . HOO-HOO, HOO-HOO-AW-AWAA." The volume, the resonance, of his voice, even from so large a bird, is remarkable, and the number of variations he composes on this one basic theme is as amazing as his vocabulary is confusing. But, as with other loquacious birds whose territory overlaps my own, the voice itself becomes familiar and I learn to know it is the barred owl speaking, regardless of what he says and that I don't understand a word of it. But I can, sometimes, get the gist of a conversation.

Owls do, unmistakably, converse. I have eavesdropped many an evening on a pair of courting owls sitting side by side on a broad limb of a big gum or white oak tree on the edge of the woods close by the house. They talk to each other in low voices, volubly, interminably, and with sounds far more meaningful to human ears than the clichéd billing and cooing of proverbial doves. I don't think it is an overactive imagination that invests the owls' low murmurings with paired sharing, for the tone of those two voices changes abruptly when a neighboring owl, of either sex, drops in for a visit. And a simple visit it often seems to be, a social exchange of polite opinion among the three or four owls gathered there. However, when a territorial squabble erupts, the insults sound choice and the threats unmistakable.

I have eavesdropped, too, on family conversations, when the mated birds bring their two or three youngsters out of the hole in the tree or the abandoned crow or hawk nest to sit with them in the early twilight on a favorite limb. There are coaxing sounds, and mildly scolding sounds, and a considerable amount of just plain fussing until they are all nicely lined up and an apparent question-and-answer period begins.

I have never seen the owlets take their first flight, nor learn to hunt, nor have I ever seen them eating anything. These activities of the young must, so far as I know, be confined to the hours of darkness, although the barred owl is not by any means a strictly nocturnal bird.

He has a tremendous ability to expand and contract the pupil aperture of his eyes so that he can see in daylight as well as in darkness. I have found him hunting—using the technique of dropping from a low limb upon a hapless mouse or a small bird feeding on the ground beneath the tree—as late as ten o'clock in the morning and as early as three o'clock in the afternoon, even on a sunny day. And he is almost as apt to give his eight-hooted call at noon as at midnight, especially on stormy winter days.

During one particular dark gray, three-day storm of misty, curtain-blowing snow, the barred owl holed up in the muffled pines to the north of the house. From this snow-hung retreat he hooted, almost without letup, six times around the clock.

He probably called from hunger, for scarcely a wild thing stirred during the storm, and his voice, which I usually enjoy hearing, became a ceaseless doom-telling: "COLD-DEATH, FROM-STORM. . . . AND-STAR-VA-TION-AW!" I was most grateful when the storm moved on, and the barred owl could go back to his normal routines of living, and to a vocabulary not so easily interpreted.

Of Winter Fogs and Hoarfrost

The fogs of January rarely steal in on little cat feet. They roll in like the tide, and they trail whole seas behind them. These are seas that billow thick and white and all-concealing over harbor and city and the countryside beyond; silent seas that muffle other sounds; unstoppable seas that slow the commerce of man—until the fog moves on.

And January fogs are in no hurry to move. They thin or vanish in the middle of the day, like the tide gone out, and return with the setting of the sun for a week or more at a time. January fogs can hang on horizons all the day and roll in slowly and inexorably when darkness falls, or they can suddenly and dramatically engulf the daylight world.

On a January morning, several years ago, following a series of such fogs that came soon after a deep-drifting snow, the sun rose clear and bright against a cloudless sky. Stark black tree-trunks forested the woodlands, diamonds and sapphires danced from the snowdrifts, and the clefts in the hills were deep in blue shadows.

The thermometer read fifteen degrees, and Kela and I, starting our morning walk, crunched through frozen snow that covered grasses and stones and all the little game trails in forests and fields.

We visited the den of a red fox in a high outcropping and were crossing the ravine below it when a haze began to rise from the bulge of the hill ahead of us. We had scarcely taken two more steps before it became a wall of fog, thick and white and cottony. I stopped in amazement. Kela stopped, too; not, I think, because I stopped, but to watch it for herself. In moments it stretched the entire length of the field and increased in height from probably one foot, when I first noticed it, to eight feet or ten. It materialized out of nothingness, a fog suddenly there where it had not been an instant before.

And suddenly there was no longer a wall in front of us. We were, ourselves, engulfed. We stood in a bowl, white-bottomed, white-walled, white-lidded, and there was no up or down or sideways.

Imagine a fog like this on a western prairie! I tried to frighten myself with the thought of being lost in a vast, unmarked space. I ignored the clear path of our footprints in the snow, which, however meandering, would lead to our own front door, and mentally tried my trackless wilderness. Fifty yards below us was a fence which, if followed in one direction, would lead to a neighbor's barn, and, if followed in the other, would lead to our own woods; and if we followed the far edge of the woods we'd come to our own backyard. No matter which way we walked from that spot, I realized, we'd come to a neighbor's buildings, or our own woods, or the county road. We were safe.

I suspect we would have been anyway, for although we walked through an opaque whiteness that smelled like steam and turned to prickly frost in our nostrils, Kela went directly to the one spot in the pasture fence where we can get through easily, and led unhesitatingly across the marsh to the creek, up the creek to the pond which we could see only in small, misty portions; and then, swiftly, up the ravine that splits the hill pasture.

Just as we topped the hill the enveloping fog rose slowly and visibly to hang a few feet above my head. I could look down the hill to the marsh and out across the hilltop to the countryside beyond. Everything lay clear and distinct under a ten-foot ceiling, and everything wore a furry coat it had not worn before the fog appeared.

Every twig, every branch, every brown leaf was rimed with spicular hoar frost. The brown stalks of goldenrod and the gray stalks of thistle that rose above the snow were coated in crystal. But not fully coated, I noticed when I examined them. Only their northern and eastern surfaces were frosted, and the frost was a thick-clustered fur of fine, long needles, crystal white. And every icy needle pointed to the northeast.

All through the fields, the woods, the clearing, I checked this orientation. On dogwood and hickory, oak and cedar, walnut and maple, on honeysuckle, aster, goldenrod and sedge, every furry spike pointed steadfastly to the northeast. There were needle rays, too, lying flat on the packed snow of our footprints, each long ray thick in the middle and tapering finely at the ends.

I phoned a meteorologist friend ten miles away. He assured me I had taken leave of my senses. "There is no fog!" he said. "There is out here," I answered, but he denied it. "I know it takes just the right set of conditions to bring all this about," I told him, "but it *has* happened. We have a fifty-foot ceiling now and the whole world out here is dressed in frost needles. Every one of those needles is at least three-eighths of an inch long, and every one of those needles is pointing toward the northeast." My friend's denials ceased and he said, very softly, into the mouthpiece, "They'd *have* to point northeast. There's a gentle airflow from the southwest."

Just as suddenly as it had come, the fog disappeared. The sun shone, and the hoarfrost vanished as though it had never been. Again, the long tree trunks stood black in the woodlands, diamonds and sapphires danced from the snowdrifts, and blue shadows marked the deep clefts in the hills.

When Life Hangs in the Balance

The February wind blew steadily from the northwest. It pushed the waters of the newly thawed pond into the upper shallows and piled them, roiling and deep, between the banks of the narrow inlet stream.

From the crest of the earth dam, my back to the wind, I watched the ceaseless running of the low gray waves to their small breaking on the upper shore, and thought of the hunger of all earth's creatures in this last dark moon of winter when supply of food and spark of life hang together at their lowest ebb.

I thought of the frogs and the tadpoles and the turtles deep in the mud of the pond bottom, lost in a winter sleep that touches the very edges of death. I thought of the fish and the snails and the whirligig beetles living sluggishly in the deepest waters in the middle of the pond. I thought of dragonfly nymphs and encysted paramecia. And I thought of muskrats alive, awake and aware through the long winter, feeding on hidden roots and bulbs, but sleeping, this windbeaten day, in their dark burrows in the banks of the pond and the stream.

At the foot of a willow tree I could see a cottontail crouched in the faint protection of sedges and briers, and, on the hilltop, a red fox slipping through the sassafras copse. How long, I wondered, until hungry rabbit and hungrier fox should meet?

When I came to the pond, the smell of wet earth rode heavily on the wind. Not the smell of freshness and wetness that speaks of coming spring, but the soggy-earth smell of a partial melt, of a winter growing slowly old but not yet over. Now, the wind took on an icy bite, thickening the surface mud, stiffening the reeds and the grasses, and turning the fine-whipped spray to crystal on the margins of the pond.

Something—a change in the wind-sound? a different smell?

—made me turn to see an opaque wall of snow advancing through the dark skeletons of the woods, obliterating trees and fence posts as it came. Up the open marsh it swept, obscuring the nearest fencerow and even the close-by willow tree at the foot of the dam before it streamed over and about me, plastering me from head to foot with wooly white, and then passed on across the pond and off to the east, whitening the earth in its swift wind-driven passage.

Following in its wake came a long-falling mist of snow-flakes, storm-shattered and fine, hiding the horizon but only graying the nearer woods and the fencerows.

On the winds made visible by the long, slanting lines of snow, two red-tailed hawks came drifting through the dark limbs of oaks and swept out above the snow-frothed marsh. Only thirty or forty feet above the sedges and the reeds, they sailed as silently and as effortlessly as the snowmist.

They cruised well apart and at an angle to one another, with the smaller bird, the male, in the lead. Their dark eyes, almost as large in diameter as a man's, scrutinized the earth beneath them for the fleetest motion, the slightest irregularity, that would betray the position of a little food animal.

A flock of juncos flitted across the marsh below the two hunters but neither one dipped a feather toward the little birds. They checked the flock for weakened members, I'm sure, but they wasted neither time nor strength pursuing the quicksilver midgets. Voles or meadow mice, the staples of their winter diet, were what they hunted—and where better to find them than in the marshes and the bordering hayfields and fencerows.

The two hawks sailed silently along, riding on the wind, wide wings and flaring tails outspread, approaching through the mist of the snow closer and closer to where I stood. I could see the whiteness of their breasts and, as they tipped on the wind, the rusty redness of their tails.

Red-tails are two years old before they acquire that signature color, two years old before they mate and nest and rear young of their own; and I have known these two as a nesting pair for four or five years, so they are not amateurs at the hunting game. But how plentiful is their food supply this winter?

This week? Today? Starvation stalks these predators as relentlessly as they stalk their smaller prey—and with greater certainty. So I watched anxiously for a swoop to the earth, closing
my heart against the bright-eyed mouse in the reeds, thinking,
rather, of destructive hordes of rodents and the thinning ranks
of hawks.

Now the male hawk, still in the lead, stopped in midair.
He hung there for measurable moments, his broad wings fanning
the snow-filled currents. Then, like a winged stone he dropped,
his talons curved sharply downward, into a clump of tawny
sedge. His wings flapped once and a fountain of snow flew up
around him.

The female hawk drew abreast of her mate. Intent on her
own hunting, she passed on as though unaware that he had
plunged. It made no difference to her. Well-fed or starving, they
never shared a kill.

But there was no kill. The male lifted himself into the air,
his curved talons as empty as his crop. With several beats of
his broad brown wings he overtook his mate and, floating
smoothly on the snow-filled wind, they swept out of the marsh
together. Up and over the pasture hill they soared, and their
dark, unfed forms vanished into the gray mists beyond.

Wildlings

Designed by Gerard A. Valerio
Composed by the Service Composition Company, Baltimore, Maryland
in Palatino with display initials in Torino
Printed by the Wolk Press, Inc., Baltimore, Maryland
on 70 lb. White Mohawk Superfine Smooth
Bound by the Optic Bindery, Inc., Glen Burnie, Maryland

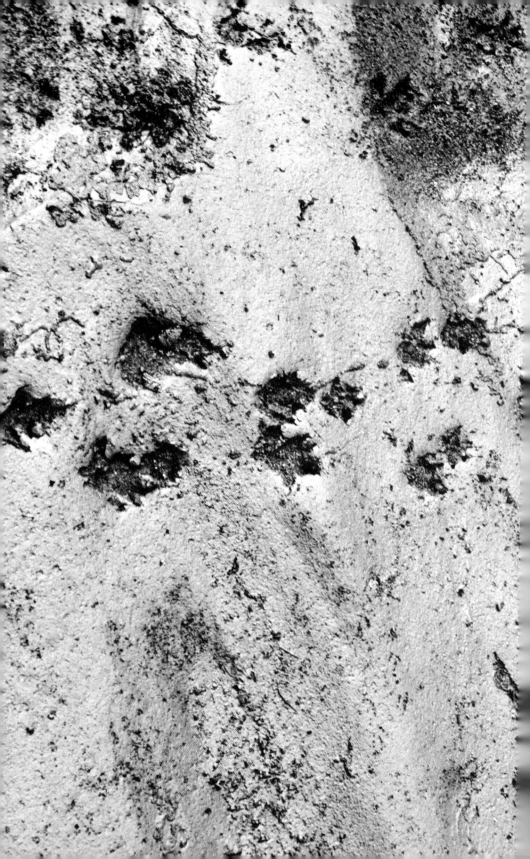